A GUIDED TOUR THROUGH HISTORY

New York Immigrant Experience

HELP US KEEP THIS GUIDE UP TO DATE

We would love to hear from you concerning your experiences with this guide and how you feel it could be improved and kept up to date. Please send your comments and suggestions to:

editorial@GlobePequot.com

Thanks for your input, and happy travels!

A Timeline Book

A GUIDED TOUR THROUGH HISTORY

New York Immigrant Experience

RANDI MINETOR

Photographs by Nic Minetor

travel

Guilford, Connecticut

An imprint of Globe Pequot Press

Original base maps provided by Compass Maps, Ltd.
Updated maps and tour maps by Nick Trotter © Morris Book Publishing, LLC.
Historical PopOut map courtesy of the Library of Congress.

All photographs © Nic Minetor except for the following: Photo on p. 3 courtesy of University of Texas Libraries; photos on pp. 5 (top), 8, 9, 11 (top and bottom), 12, 14, 16, 17, 19, 23, 26, 31, 32, 34, 40, 45, 46 (top and bottom), 48, 50, 51, 54, 56, 59, 75, 79, 81, 82, 85, and 87 courtesy of the Library of Congress; photo on p. 22 courtesy of the Statue of Liberty–Ellis Island Foundation, Inc.; and photo on p. 25 courtesy of Wikimedia Commons.

Library of Congress Cataloging-in-Publication Data

Minetor, Randi.
  New York immigrant experience : a guided tour through history / Randi Minetor ; photographs by Nic Minetor.
       p. ; cm.
  "A Timeline book."
  Includes bibliographical references (p. 132-146) and index.
  ISBN 978-0-7627-5743-5
  1. New York (N.Y.)—Tours. 2. Historic sites—New York (State)—New York—Guidebooks. 3. Historic buildings—New York (State)—New York—Guidebooks. 4. Walking—New York (State)—New York—Guidebooks. 5. Minorities—New York (State)—New York—History. 6. Immigrants—New York (State)—New York—History. 7. New York (N.Y.)—History. 8. New York (N.Y.)—Ethnic relations. I. Title.

  F128.18.M554 2010
  917.47'10444—dc22

                                                                    2009048155
Printed in China
10 9 8 7 6 5 4 3 2 1

All the information in this guidebook is subject to change. We recommend that you call ahead to obtain current information before traveling. All restaurants are open daily for breakfast, lunch, and dinner, unless otherwise noted.

Contents

Introduction

If you've come to New York to find the city's true heritage and its deep roots in a multiplicity of cultures and backgrounds, you needn't go far to find it: Spend a few minutes standing on a street corner in any of the five boroughs, and count the number of languages, the many styles of dress, and the palette of skin tones that whiz by.

Stand on any street corner in Manhattan to experience the city's heritage.

Today, 60 percent of New York City's residents are either immigrants or children of immigrants who came to this city in search of a new way of living—the potential for prosperity, an escape from persecution, the freedom to enjoy basic human rights, or the possibility of peaceful coexistence with people of different races, ages, religions, or political beliefs.

As recently as 2005, more than 36 percent of New York City's residents were born on foreign soil, a fitting tribute to the days when ships crossed the ocean to carry five thousand passengers a day into the city's ports. The vast immigration of the late nineteenth and early twentieth centuries has long passed, but its spirit echoes up and down New York's streets and throughout its businesses, mercantile districts, skyscrapers, shops, restaurants, museums, theaters, and apartments. The taxi driver who carries you across town may be of Middle Eastern or Indian descent; the street vendor handing you a hot dog and a bottle of water is as likely to be Nigerian as Irish or German; the grocers who offer fresh produce, meat, and fish may be Chinese, Taiwanese, Bangladeshi, or Korean; the city's most popular bakeries are owned by Italian, French, Jewish, or Eastern European citizens and infused with recipes passed down through a dozen generations.

Grocers and food vendors come from dozens of countries around the world.

The phenomenon that historians called the "melting pot" originated here in New York, the unification of dozens of disparate cultures into one brilliant pastiche that we know as the American way of life. To blend, and become part of a cohesive whole with its own homogeneous identity, was the one major demand of immigrants in the nation's earlier days—and today third-, fourth-, and fifth-generation Americans can list half a dozen countries of origin in their lineage.

Perhaps this is exactly why we return to New York City to explore the immigration stories of the nineteenth and twentieth century, searching for kernels of authenticity beyond the cultural blend. We come sleuthing for clues about our grandparents' and great-grandparents' experiences as newcomers, living in a land that expected them to learn the language, pull themselves up by their bootstraps, fill their own larders, and pay their own way in their struggle for the American dream. Nowhere in America can we learn more about that experience than in New York, where ethnic neighborhoods retain the cultural identity they adopted a century and a half ago, and edifices constructed to welcome, question, house, shepherd, feed, and sometimes try and convict these immigrants still stand throughout Lower Manhattan and nearby islands.

Diversity for Fair Trade

The first inklings of a land open to all came well before the founding fathers gathered in Philadelphia. Back in 1613, the Dutch arrived in what they dubbed New Netherland, the area that would become New York State, bringing with them a long-held philosophy of fair trade with whomever could purchase their wares. They established a fur trading settlement on the island

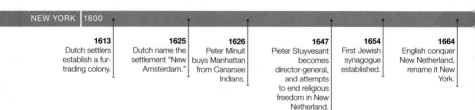

NEW YORK | 1600

1613	1625	1626	1647	1654	1664
Dutch settlers establish a fur-trading colony.	Dutch name the settlement "New Amsterdam."	Peter Minuit buys Manhattan from Canarsee Indians.	Pieter Stuyvesant becomes director-general, and attempts to end religious freedom in New Netherland.	First Jewish synagogue established.	English conquer New Netherland, rename it New York.

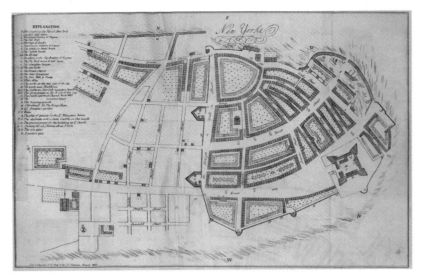

Map of New York, 1695.

the resident native people—a subgroup of Lenape Indians known as the Canarsee—called "Manna-hatta," or "Island of Hills." By 1625, the Dutch newcomers had renamed the trading post New Amsterdam. The following year, Dutch merchant Peter Minuit purchased Manhattan Island from the Canarsee, in a transaction that has undergone significant retelling and revision in the ensuing years (see the sidebar on page 4).

The Dutch saw the New World's commercial potential, enthusiastically embracing its ability to open up new trade avenues with people from all over Europe and Africa. To this end, the leaders of the Dutch West India Company—sponsors of this early exploration—opened its colony to people

1700

1690s
African Burial Ground established in downtown Manhattan.

1748
20 percent of New York City population is African.

1776
United States declares its independence from England.

1783
U.S. wins Revolutionary War.

1786
Irish immigrants found Tammany Society.

1789
French Revolution and Napoleonic Wars begin.

$24 in Trinkets? The Real Story of the Manhattan Purchase

Generations of popular wisdom have told us that Peter Minuit purchased the 22,000 acres of Manhattan Island from the Canarsee Indians for a handful of trinkets, valued at somewhere around $24. History tells us otherwise, however: We can gain some perspective from the work of modern-day historians Edwin G. Burroughs and Mike Wallace.

It turns out that an official letter recorded the transaction back in 1626, written by Pieter Janszoon Schagen, a member of the board of the Dutch West India Company. The goods traded for Manhattan are not listed in the letter, but shortly thereafter, Minuit closed a transaction to purchase Staten Island in which he traded iron kettles, axe heads, bolts of cloth, farming implements, and "other wares." We are safe in assuming that Minuit bought Manhattan with the same kind of items to trade. All of these tools and dry goods would have been more than desirable to the Indians, as they represented the latest in seventeenth-century European technology.

The actual value of the trade, according to Schagen's letter, was 60 guilders—or about $1,000 in today's U.S. dollars. The $24 figure most likely came from a narrative written in 1846, in which a New York historian made the conversion based on a flawed comparison of Dutch and American currency—but the outlandish figure became part of the culture, and remains so to this day.

4

of all backgrounds and religious orientations to come to New Netherland and become part of an exciting new revenue stream.

Settlers from other nations believed that New Netherland would welcome them indefinitely—and by the mid-1600s, seventeen languages were spoken in the town of New Amsterdam alone as people flocked there from all over Europe and northern Africa. The tolerance settlers found when they arrived, however, turned out to be short-lived.

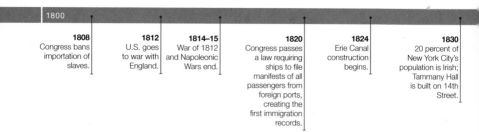

1800					
1808 Congress bans importation of slaves.	**1812** U.S. goes to war with England.	**1814–15** War of 1812 and Napoleonic Wars end.	**1820** Congress passes a law requiring ships to file manifests of all passengers from foreign ports, creating the first immigration records.	**1824** Erie Canal construction begins.	**1830** 20 percent of New York City's population is Irish; Tammany Hall is built on 14th Street.

Pieter Stuyvesant became director-general in 1647.

In 1647, Pieter Stuyvesant became director-general of the colony of New Netherland, a position he would hold until 1664. His first order of business was to put an end to religious freedom in the new colony, specifically banning the Jews from living in New Netherland. What the new governor had not taken into account, however, was that several board members of the Dutch West India Company were Sephardic Jews from Spain and Portugal, with significant interests in the New World colony. The Company quickly interceded, rescinding Stuyvesant's new edict and welcoming anyone who could help the colony grow and prosper. In 1654, a group of Sephardic Jewish settlers, fleeing persecution from the new Portuguese rulers of Brazil, established the first official Jewish congregation in New Amsterdam: Congregation Shearith Israel, now located at 8 West 70th Street at Central Park West. The congregation's cemetery—the oldest Jewish burial ground in the United

The oldest Jewish cemetery in New York resides at Chatham Square and St. James Place.

1830s	1840s	1845	1848	1850s	1858
207,000 Irish, 76,000 English, and 152,000 Germans arrive in New York.	Ashkenazi Jews from Germany begin to arrive in U.S.	Irish potato famine begins; 350,000 people die in the next two years. Nearly 2 million Irish depart for America.	German revolution fails; more than 1 million Germans come to U.S. Chinese immigrants begin to arrive in California for the Gold Rush.	Irish, Italian, and Chinese immigrants populate Five Points; gang violence there is considered worst in the world.	William M. "Boss" Tweed becomes grand sachem of Tammany Hall.

The African Burial Ground: An Astonishing Discovery in Downtown Manhattan

In 1991, before the construction of the federal office building at 290 Broadway, an archeological excavation revealed the remains of a cemetery more than 350 years old. Records from the 1700s noted that the cemetery was there and that it was a burial ground for African slaves, but so much excavation and construction had taken place in this busy area—just down the road from New York City Hall—that officials considered it long destroyed. To everyone's amazement, archeologists disinterred the remains of hundreds of bodies in less than an acre of the 6.6-acre burial ground. Further excavation halted as scholars, anthropologists, and area residents took up the cause of the burial ground's preservation, battling developers whose contractual demands made them anxious to keep construction on schedule.

It took years, several congressional hearings, and the actions of many concerned citizens to interrupt a $30- to $40-million construction project and remove the remains, but in the end, the African Burial Ground was declared a national monument and was placed under the protection of the National Park Service. Construction resumed after archeologists had removed 419 sets of remains, which were reinterred at the site after the building was finished. These

remains now lay under a series of mounds as part of the sleek, symbolic memorial that stands on the burial site today. The national monument visitor center, on the first floor of 290 Broadway, shows an eye-opening 25-minute video that details the history of slaves in New York. Visitor center: M–F 9–5, free. Memorial: M–Su 9–5, closed Thanksgiving, Christmas, and New Year's Day.

1865	1868	1869	1870	1875	1878	1880s
Civil War ends. More than a quarter of New York's population is Irish immigrants.	Burlingame Treaty allows Chinese and U.S. citizens to migrate freely between the two countries.	12,000 Chinese complete western half of transcontinental railroad.	Boss Tweed becomes New York City's commissioner of public works.	Page Act forbids Asian women considered "obnoxious" to leave their homelands for U.S.	First Chinese grocer opens on Mott Street. U.S. Supreme Court denies Chinese the right to become American citizens.	Pogroms drive Jews from Russian Empire.

States—remains at the synagogue's original location, at St. James Place off of Chatham Square on Manhattan's Lower East Side.

Under Stuyvesant's management, the population of slaves brought from Africa increased as rapidly as did the white residency in New Amsterdam—by 1660, the settlement had established the largest population of urban slaves in North America. No strangers to the slave trade, the Dutch West India Company began bringing Africans to America as early as 1626, capturing them from Portuguese and Spanish ships during a war that began in 1621. Pressed into service by their captors, these slaves can be credited with construction of the first buildings in New Amsterdam and production of many of the goods sold by the Dutch West India Company; they also played a role in the defense of the Dutch colony against Native Americans.

The Conquering English

When the English set their sights on conquest of New Netherland in September 1664, it took no time at all for the stronger military power to take the colony away from its original settlers. Colonel Richard Nicolls and a handful of English frigates arrived in the harbor, gaining reinforcements from New Englanders living on Long Island—and when Nicolls demanded New Netherland's immediate surrender, Stuyvesant found himself alone in his resistance as his citizens declined to back up his defense. The director-general had no choice but to hand over the city and the whole of the Dutch colony to the British usurpers in an entirely bloodless coup.

The Dutch continued to contest England's conquest for another ten years, but in 1674, with its resources depleted, the Dutch agreed to cede the colony

1882	1886	1890	1890s	1892	1898
Chinese Exclusion Act prohibits Chinese from entering U.S.	Statue of Liberty inaugurated.	Richard Croker becomes leader of Tammany Hall.	450,000 Greeks begin to arrive, escaping Ottoman rule and the Balkan Wars.	Ellis Island opens to receive immigrants.	*U.S. v. Wong Kim Ark:* Supreme Court decides that a child born in the U.S. is a U.S. citizen.

The English took New Amsterdam from Stuyvesant easily in 1664.

to English rule, receiving in return the South American country we now know as Suriname. The Dutch withdrew from New Netherland—renamed New York by the English—and turned their attentions much farther south, to the country's holdings in and around the Caribbean Sea.

With England in charge, the migration across the ocean from Europe notched significantly upward. The population of New York City grew from 6,000 to more than 33,000 over the next century, filling its streets with English settlers and merchants as well as people from many other European countries. More people meant a need for more infrastructure—particularly housing—and a greater need for labor to clear land, build apartment buildings and houses, create roads and construct shops and markets.

The answer: Solicit able-bodied Europeans to come to America, where they were promised steady work in a land of adventure and the opportunity to seek their fortunes. In particular, the government reached out to German Protestants in 1708, arranging passage to the New World through London for 13,500 Germans. (Notably, the English turned back 2,257 Roman Catholic Germans, once again making it clear that religious freedom extended only to those of "acceptable" faiths.)

1900

1900
More than 484,000 Italians have arrived in New York. U.S. has third largest Jewish population in the world (about 1.5 million).

1901
Tenement House Act brings first housing reforms.

1905
Poles arrive en masse, escaping racist persecution and unemployment.

1910
Triangle Shirtwaist Factory fire.

1918–19
El Barrio (Spanish Harlem) becomes New York's first significant Latino community.

1920
More than 4 million Italians have immigrated to U.S. Nearly 23 percent of the world's Jews live in U.S.

The rosy picture of wealth and promise the English painted did not materialize for most of the Germans. The process of transporting these people to America took six months, and many died of typhus during the crossing. Those who managed to survive the tempestuous ocean voyage were quickly discouraged from seeking a living in New York City when confronted with its filth and congestion, so most of the Germans moved upstate, settling

Immigrants took their lives in hand when they boarded ocean-bound ships.

along the southern bank of the Mohawk River and forming towns that stand today, including Manheim and Herkimer, NY. Others moved west and south into Pennsylvania, where they established a strong agricultural community.

The Irish fell prey to a similar English scheme, choosing to leave their homeland for America as a population boom swept through Ireland in the mid-1700s, producing more mouths to feed than there was food for their nourishment. Hoping for a better life in the New World, they took advantage of dirt-cheap fares offered by the English to make the crossing, but they were not prepared for the nightmarish conditions their neighbors to the south would proffer for them. The boats came to be called "coffin ships," carrying nearly as many men to their deaths as to America—and friends and neighbors in Ireland took to giving their loved ones an "American wake" before they set sail, acknowledging the fact that many would not survive the crossing, let alone return to Ireland with money in their pockets.

1924	1929	1933	1935	1939	1941	1943
National Origins Quota Act and Immigration Act: first annual immigration quotas established; Asians and Asian Indians banned from immigration to U.S. Johnson-Reed Act bans people from Eastern Europe from coming into the U.S.	Governor Franklin Roosevelt launches Home Relief.	Fiorello LaGuardia, an Italian-American, becomes mayor of New York City.	New law requires all wooden stairways be replaced with metal; tenements begin to close down.	SS St. Louis sails for Cuba, but is turned away at port; U.S. also rejects the ship of 930 German Jews.	U.S. enters World War II.	Magnuson Act repeals laws against Chinese immigration.

Adding insult to injury, the ships that carried the Irish to America did not make landfall in New York, but sailed for the Canadian coast—and the passengers received no transportation southward to the promised jobs. Some took freighters to Boston or New York, while others simply walked south until they reached a community with a strong Irish population.

With the coming of the Revolutionary War in America, however, new arrivals from Europe slowed to a trickle, and the world watched to see if a fledgling nation conceived in liberty could stand against the monarchical British machine and the massive forces of England's allies.

A New Nation's "Golden Door"

The United States' victory against England in the Revolutionary War in 1783 signaled sweeping change in America, but the details of that change would take decades to sort out and put into practice. Meanwhile, Europe turned its attention to the French Revolution and the Napoleonic Wars, conscripting huge armies of men into military service and curtailing immigration until well into the nineteenth century. By the time Napoleon was forced out of Russian territory in December 1812, the United States had become embroiled in a second war against the English—this one over British restrictions that interfered with American's trade relations with France, while England essentially kidnapped American citizens and forced them to serve in the Royal Navy. It wasn't until the Treaty of Ghent was signed between the United States and England in December 1814, and the last fighting finally died away in early 1815, that the U.S. could safely open its ports to immigration once again.

By this time only about 100,000 people living in the United States had not

1944	1945	1952	1959	1965	1966
War Refugee Board permits civilian victims of WWII to immigrate to U.S.	Congress passes War Bride Act and GI Fiancées Act.	Immigration and National-ity Act allows naturalization regardless of race.	Castro's Cuban revolution prompts 200,000 people to emigrate to U.S.	Hart-Cellar Immigration and Nationality Act abolishes racial quotas for immigration.	Cuban Refugee Readjustment Act allows 400,000 fleeing Cubans to enter U.S.

been born on American soil—barely 1 percent of the new nation's 8.3 million citizens. Already its major cities were becoming hubs of importation and commerce, bringing goods from countries in Europe and beyond into the fledgling country. Only a few

The War of 1812, fought primarily at sea, slowed immigration to America.

years earlier, in 1803, President Thomas Jefferson and a team of diplomats and negotiators bought a swath of land from Napoleon that doubled the size of the United States, creating a vast new frontier that only a handful of worthy explorers—led by Meriwether Lewis and William Clark—had begun to navigate and map. More land meant more settlement, a greater need to build new means of transporting goods and resources, and more opportunity for

the world's poor, downtrodden, and underprivileged to find their way to fortune.

Between 1815 and 1820, with the wars' aftermath winding down and new issues of hunger and poverty surfacing in Europe, the mass exodus to the United States began.

Captains Lewis and Clark hold a council with the Indians.

				2000	
1968 Quotas raised for Chinese immigrants.	**1980** New York's Chinatown becomes largest concentration of Chinese Americans in U.S.	**1990** 24.4 percent of New York City's population is Hispanic.	**1991** African Burial Ground redis- covered during excavation for construction of an office building.	**2000** Largest immigrant populations are now Asian, Caribbean, and Hispanic/ Latino (mostly Dominican).	**2009** New York City has the largest population of black immigrants in the country: more than 686,000. More than 690,000 New Yorkers are of Italian descent. Immigrant popula- tions now fill the suburbs.

Key Participants in New York Immigration History

Richard Croker Carrying on the unfortunate legacy bequeathed to him by William M. Tweed and his cronies, the Irish-born Croker led Tammany Hall according to the old tradition: by accepting bribes from prostitution rings, saloons, and halls where illegal gambling took place. His willingness to look the other way for money soon made him a rich man, a feat he had not achieved as an alderman from 1868 to 1870, as coroner from 1873 to 1876, or as city chamberlain from 1889 to 1890. Through Croker's support and influence, Robert A. Van Wyck became the first mayor of the united five boroughs of New York—and historians assume that Croker essentially ran the city, through the politician he'd chosen as his front man. When his power and influence failed to elect Edward M. Shepard, the mayoral candidate he'd selected, in 1901, Croker resigned from Tammany Hall and retired to his native Ireland, living out his days in the quiet countryside.

John Gotti, Jr. The most flamboyant and powerful of the organized-crime leaders that made Little Italy a notorious mob base, Gotti led the Gambino crime family until his conviction in 1992 on thirteen counts of murder, as well as racketeering, obstruction of justice, conspiracy to commit murder, illegal gambling, extortion, tax evasion, and loan-sharking. The FBI finally caught up with Gotti through an electronic surveillance operation involving wiretapping and taping of discussions in an apartment above the Ravenite Social Club in Little Italy. He was arrested in a raid at the Ravenite on December 11, 1990, along with two other mob leaders, convicted in April 1992, and sentenced to life in prison with no parole. Gotti died in prison of throat cancer on June 10, 2002.

Sender Jarmulowsky The impressive stone building on the corner of Orchard and Canal Streets bears the name of S. Jarmulowsky, the man who founded a bank on the Lower East Side in 1873 and built this proud edifice in 1912. A Russian immigrant and self-made wealthy philanthropist, Jarmulowsky applied his sound business sense to his dealings with customers, connecting with them on the basis of their character rather than on their current financial position. His strategy worked—the bank remained strong and solvent until his death in 1912, barely a month after the bank moved into the new building. In just a few years' time, his two sons, who took over the bank at the time of his death, managed to run the business into the ground.

Fiorello LaGuardia Mayor of New York City from 1934 to 1945, LaGuardia was the first Italian-American to hold the post and a true advocate for the enormous immigrant population whose heritage he shared. An advocate for the poor of every color and background, LaGuardia supported President Roosevelt's New Deal and led New York to recovery from the Great Depression. In the dramatic initial moments of his first term in office, LaGuardia ordered the arrest of mob boss Lucky Luciano, whose criminal reign in Little Italy

Fiorello LaGuardia (left) and NLRB chair J. Warren Madden

had painted the entire Italian population with the gangster's brush. He continued his rally against organized crime by rounding up Frank Costello and his thousands of illegal slot machines, and ensuring that Luciano was tried and convicted for his leadership of a citywide prostitution ring. (Luciano received a 30- to 50-year sentence.) Later, he ordered "slum clearance," tearing down the tenements and the elevated train tracks on the Lower East Side and putting thousands of immigrants to work in the city's parks through a massive public works program. In 1946, after his last term as mayor, LaGuardia became the director-general for the United Nations Relief and Rehabilitation Administration.

Peter Minuit A Walloon from Wesel (today's north-ern Germany), Minuit served as director-general of the Dutch Colony of New Netherland from 1626 to 1633. He made the actual purchase of Manhattan Island from the Canarsee Indians—a band of the Lenape tribe—in 1626, trading goods that were valued at 60 Dutch guilders at the time, or about $1,000 in today's U.S. dollars. The details of the transaction were set down in a letter by a board member of the Dutch West India Company.

Annie Moore The first immigrant ever to set foot on Ellis Island on January 1, 1892, fifteen-year-old Annie Moore arrived on the steamship *Nevada* from County Cork, Ireland, along with 147 other steerage passengers. She and her fellow travelers moved from the *Nevada* to an immigrant transfer boat, the *John E. Moore,* which was decorated for the occasion with bunting and all the bells and whistles—literally—and the carefully chosen young woman was whisked into the main building, registered, and presented with a ten-dollar gold piece by Colonel John B. Weber, local superintendent of immigration. Annie and her two brothers went on to join their parents, who lived at 32 Monroe Street in New York City. It's only recently that Annie's continued story as an immigrant and American citizen came to light: While many people (including historians at Ellis Island) believed that she had moved west to Indiana, New Mexico, and Texas, and had perished in a streetcar accident in 1924, that story turned out to be about a different Annie Moore. Research conducted in 2006 revealed that Ellis Island's Annie actually remained in New York City, marrying Joseph Augustus Schayer in 1895 and bearing eleven children. She died of heart failure in 1924 at 99 Cherry Street in New York.

Colonel Richard Nicolls Nicolls received an appointment from the Duke of York in 1664 to lead an expedition to New England and conquer New Netherland, bringing the Dutch colony into line with the British holdings to its north and east. When he and his fellow frigate commanders arrived on the shores of New Netherland on September 8, they found Director-General Pieter Stuyvesant undefended and the colony ripe for the taking. Nicolls renamed the colony New York and remained as the first English deputy-governor, restoring religious freedom and guaranteeing property rights for its residents. He continued as the on-the-ground official in New York until 1668, when he returned to England.

Jacob Riis The author and photographer of the landmark volume *How the Other Half Lives: Studies Among the Tenements of New York* began his career as a carpenter, discovering firsthand how miserable the life of an immigrant could be in New York City. He arrived in New York from his native Denmark in 1870 and spent many nights on the street, homeless and hungry like so many of the people around him. Finally, after three years of the transient life, he landed a position as a police reporter, rising to the *New York Tribune* and the New York bureau of the Associated Press in 1877. With a beat that took him to Mulberry Street and into the heart of the east-side slums day and night, Riis saw what most New Yorkers managed to ignore: thousands of people living in filth and depravity, with no hope for improvement of their situations. What he saw turned him into a crusader for the rights of these immigrants, using his work for the AP and the *Tribune* as a bully pulpit to expose landlords for criminal neglect of the tenements, inadequate laws for failing to provide for human beings living in depravity, and the general public for turning away from the poor and indigent. Thanks to Riis's work, reforms were set in motion that brought humane changes to tenement life.

Franklin D. Roosevelt Before he became the thirty-second president of the United States, Franklin Roosevelt served as governor of New York, presiding over the state as the stock market crashed in October 1929. Moving quickly to take care of the people who needed the greatest assistance, Roosevelt launched a program called Home

New York Immigrant Experience

Relief, supplying government funds to the poor in the form of rent-payment subsidies and food and opening the state's surplus stored in warehouses to provide cheese, flour, and other necessities to the poor. His innate empathy for the plight of the state's downtrodden would pave the way for his election to the presidency in 1932. As president he continued in a similar vein, creating the Federal Emergency Relief Administration, Social Security, the Public Works Administration, the Federal Deposit Insurance Corporation, the Farm Credit Administration, the Civil Works Administration and the Works Progress Administration—all programs to aid the poor, put people to work, and protect the money they earned and saved in banks.

Alexander T. Stewart An Irish-born American with extraordinary business sense, Stewart joined his mother in New York City when he was fifteen and opened his first dry goods store when he was twenty, using money he had inherited from his grandfather that year. The original 12.5-by-30-foot space never wore a sign, but Stewart's salesmanship and his understanding of his customers' desire for bargains made him one of the most successful businessmen in New York. Soon A. T. Stewart & Company became the father of all department stores, allowing its owner to build his famous "Marble Palace," a marble-fronted store that still stands at 280 Broadway, and making Stewart a rich man. He prospered further by inventing the mail-order business, responding to letters from women all over the country and sending them the merchandise they requested—setting the standard for Sears, Montgomery Ward, and Spiegel. In 1869–70, Stewart built the first of what would become known as the Fifth Avenue palaces, a marble-covered, three-story home with a mansard roof in the French Second Empire style, on the northwest corner of 34th Street. (That structure was razed in 1901.)

Pieter Stuyvesant Director-general of New Netherland from 1647 to 1664, Stuyvesant was the last Dutch official to preside over the New World colony. Under his jurisdiction, the settlement of New Amsterdam expanded beyond Mannattan's southern tip, and he used African slaves and some Dutchmen to build the wall that gave Wall Street its name—a stockade that defined the northern boundary of New Amsterdam, constructed to ward off Indian attacks. Stuyvesant lost his right leg in a battle for the island of Saint Martin in 1644, before he began his tenure in New Netherland; in his next battle, a bloodless coup for ownership of New Netherland, he lost the colony to the English.

William M. "Boss" Tweed One of the most powerful men in New York, Tweed led the Irish political machine based at Tammany Hall after serving in the U.S. House of Representatives and on the New York City Board of Advisors. As New York commissioner of public works, a position he assumed in 1870, Tweed took control of the city's municipal government and carried out an extensive fraud operation that bilked millions of dollars from the city's taxpayers. A *New York Times* exposé and the determination of reformer William H. Wickham finally led to Tweed's undoing in October 1871, when he was arrested and held on $8 million bail; a conviction followed two years later. The story didn't end there, however: A higher court reduced his twelve-year sentence to one year, putting Tweed back on the street after a comparatively short incarceration. He could not be tried again for criminal activity, but New York City sued him for $6 million, landing him in debtors' prison. Unable to post the $3 million bail required for his release, Tweed managed to escape the prison and fled to Spain . . . but the Spanish government returned him to New York, where he died of pneumonia in the Ludlow Street Jail in 1878.

William H. Wickham A diamond merchant and career volunteer fireman who became president of the New York Fire Department in 1860, Wickham became the Democratic leader of the opposition to Boss Tweed's embezzlement schemes in the early 1870s. As chairman of the Apollo Hall Democracy, he exposed Tweed's accounting practices and became a symbol for honesty and justice in New York government, handily winning the next mayoral election with the help of a newly reformed Tammany Hall. He served as New York's mayor for two years, declining to run again in 1876 and moving instead to serve on the Board of Education.

Key Participants

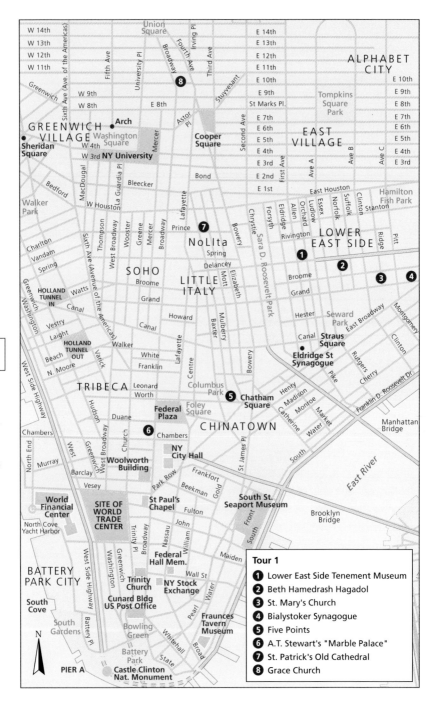

Tour 1

1. Lower East Side Tenement Museum
2. Beth Hamedrash Hagadol
3. St. Mary's Church
4. Bialystoker Synagogue
5. Five Points
6. A.T. Stewart's "Marble Palace"
7. St. Patrick's Old Cathedral
8. Grace Church

Tour 1: 1820–1870

New York: The Great Escape From Poverty and Persecution

Before 1820 the United States kept no official
records of the number of immigrants who entered
the country—in fact, the original U.S. Constitu-
tion only notes that Congress has the power "to
establish a uniform rule of naturalization," with no
specifics about what such a citizenship law might
be. Once the European wars had ended in the
mid-1810s, however, people from many countries
began to seek new homes in America, where they
believed they would find better opportunities than
those they faced in their homelands. The sheer
volume of new arrivals became so great that Congress saw the need to begin to monitor this influx
of potential citizens, perhaps with an eye toward
regulating immigration in the future.

So it was that in 1820, Congress passed a law
that required masters of ships to file a manifest
that contained a list of all passengers who had
embarked from a foreign port. The list had to
include each passenger's name, age, sex, occu-
pation, country of origin, and final destination, as
well as a list of any deaths that occurred during the
voyage.

For the first time, the United States had proper
immigration records and a way to calculate and
codify the number of people who entered the
country, where they came from, and where they
planned to go once they reached America. Over
the next ten years, these lists revealed what

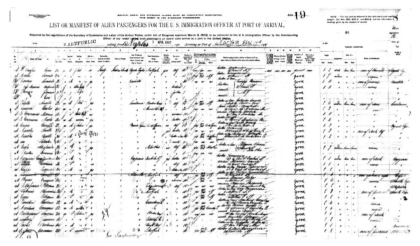

A new law required all ships to record the names and origins of their emigrating passengers.

lawmakers could see but could not calculate until then: The number of immigrants to the United States grew every year, nearly tripling in the course of the first decade for which there are records. In 1820, 8,385 immigrants entered the country; by 1830 the annual number increased to 23,322.

What made so many people brave a tumultuous, potentially deadly voyage across the Atlantic Ocean to seek their fortunes in a new, unfamiliar nation? The promise of steady work for reasonable wages caught the attention of thousands of strong, healthy men who endured miserable working conditions and poverty-level pay in their home countries.

Farm workers in Ireland faced one of the most challenging situations in Europe. Most Irish citizens earned their living by farming land that was under control of English landowners, the vast majority of whom lived in England rather than on their Irish property. These owners rented their land to small farmers, who eked out a living using antiquated

"There are several kinds of power working at the fabric of the republic—water-power, steam-power and Irish-power. The last works hardest of all."

—E. M. Johnson, Irish journalist, 1860

tools and the most primitive of methods, because they were unable to afford better. For their trouble, these laborers received just eight pence a day, a pittance even in the early 1800s—and a fraction of what they heard they could earn in America.

Eager to improve their living conditions, feed their families, and earn a chance at a more comfortable life, the Irish were among the first to sail for the United States, launching the first ship packed with 6,000 immigrants as early as 1816. By 1830, the Irish represented one-fifth of New York City's residents—and even more Irishmen moved eastward, taking jobs on a project to build a connecting waterway between the Hudson River and Lake Erie. "Clinton's Ditch," the brainchild of New York Governor Dewitt Clinton and the laughingstock of many New York (city and state) residents, proved to be far less foolhardy than scoffers first guessed: The Erie Canal became the catalyst for explosive growth in New York City, turning the town into the nation's most significant importation and shipping hub.

In the 1830s, England's monarchs recognized the trends in population growth that signaled future shortages in food and resources in Ireland, and reduced the travel restrictions on its holdings in the United Kingdom. By 1845 more than 207,000 Irish citizens had arrived in United States, taking jobs in law enforcement and fire protection, constructing Catholic churches and filling the Lower East Side's two-story apartment houses. Some 76,000 English people set sail for America during this period as well, most of them moving into New York's burgeoning uptown.

With so many Irish people making New York their home, civic-minded individuals began to

"We are starving," says the Irish herald as she waves to American ships.

St. Patrick's Old Cathedral was an early masterpiece constructed by immigrants.

realize how powerful this group could become politically. They became members of the Society of Saint Tammany, a social club and patriotic organization for middle-class Protestants founded in 1786, named for an Indian chief of the Delaware tribe around whom considerable mythology had developed during the Revolutionary War. While the original spirit of the organization remained, the "saint" was dropped from the name as more Irishmen joined in the late 1820s, and Tammany Hall was built on 14th Street in 1830 (the building is now the New York Film Academy). Tammany Hall soon became a political affiliate of the city's Democratic Party, and earned the loyalty of the Irish immigrant community as it sent "ward bosses" into the residential neighborhoods to gather votes. By 1845, the name Tammany Hall became synonymous with the vast political machine that Democrats had assembled in New York.

From Every Corner of Europe

While the Irish quickly rose to dominance in New York City in the 1830s, they were far from the only Europeans arriving by the tens of thousands. In the 1830s, 152,000 Germans came to America, part of a trend that had begun as early as 1745, when 45,000 Germans came to the English colonies in the New World and settled in Pennsylvania. Marauding armies from several countries wrought havoc on southwestern Germany throughout the 1700s and into the 1800s, making it nearly impossible to live peaceably or to earn a decent living. Modern conveniences and processes replaced many of their traditional industries, eliminating jobs for many workers while pushing many small

Revolutions in the German states failed in 1848, despite wide public support.

businesses into bankruptcy. At the same time, steam engines made it faster and cheaper for Germans to reach ocean-bound ships in England by steamboat and train.

In 1848, when the German revolution failed, more than a million Germans left their homeland for America. Newly arrived German immigrants made for the midwestern territories and Texas, where they could make their living as farmers or live in smaller towns and cities, working as cabinetmakers and machinists. German immigrants also brought to America their expertise in making some of the world's best lager beer. Soon Davenport, Iowa; Milwaukee, Wisconsin; Chicago, Illinois; and Cincinnati, Ohio, became major German destinations.

Immigrants sailed from England to America in search of a more prosperous life.

Even with the vast migration to the Midwest, more than 100,000 Germans remained in New York City in 1860, gathering in the area we now know as Alphabet City in East Greenwich Village. In just a few years, they established 20 churches, 50 schools, and two daily German-language newspapers.

Another population of German immigrants arrived as well: Ashkenazi Jews began to move from Europe to the United States in the 1840s. The term Ashkenazi refers to the geographic area in western Germany, on both sides of the river Rhine. Many of these immigrants were liberal Jews who believed in an enlightened Jewish movement known as Haskalah and saw the value in becoming part of modern Western society. Before Haskalah, Jews lived in segregation in most eastern European communities, separated from the neighboring Catholics and Protestants by their traditional clothing, language—mostly Yiddish—and the observance of Jewish Shabbos (Shabbat) and holidays that differed from modern European culture. Eager to make a living in a place that did not exclude them for being different, these Jews sought increased education in secular subjects, an opportunity to study religious texts beyond the Torah (the Old Testament), and fluency in languages beyond the Yiddish they spoke at home. This new desire for integration eventually led to the creation of denominations in the Jewish religion, the most popular of which was Reform Judaism—a movement that began in the United States. Study of secular languages allowed Jews to become part of the greater world around them, ending the isolation under which Jews lived in the "old country."

While integration with secular society was of critical importance to the newly arrived Jewish immigrants, this tightly knit community did not give up on the traditions that had allowed them to survive so long as an insular society. German Jews established *landsmanschaftn*, organizations of Jews from the same town or region, which became the social, cultural, and economic hub of New York Jewish neighborhoods. By the end of the nineteenth century, thousands of *landsmanschaftn* throughout New York provided some financial assistance to immigrant families in dire need.

Blight, Famine, and America's New Lower Class

In 1845, tragedy struck across Ireland: A blight wiped out three-quarters of the country's potato crop, the primary source of nourishment for more than half of Ireland's swelling population. The following year, the same blight struck again. In 1846 and 1847, an estimated 350,000 people died of starvation and typhus, and the end to the rampant deaths was at least another year's harvest away.

Only one option remained to the people who had managed to survive the potato famine. Nearly two million Irish citizens—about a quarter of the country's total population—left their country for America, most knowing they would never see their homeland again.

They arrived in New York penniless, their resources depleted by the cost of the voyage; poverty kept most of these people just a few blocks from Castle Garden, the port of entry at which immigrants were screened and registered

St. Mary's Church on Grand Street was one of the first Catholic churches to serve the growing Irish community.

"Cleanliness is essential to the health and comfort of steerage passengers, and should be particularly attended to. It is the custom on board of well-regulated ships, for the chief mate to see that the passengers wash out the steerage twice a week, or oftener. That is a rule of great importance, especially in warm weather; and no one should complain of the inconvenience to which it puts him. Besides this, each person should thoroughly sweep his own premises every day, and give it an occasional scrubbing with a damp mop, not a wet one; for the latter might make the steerage uncomfortable. . . . We have advised a large supply of vinegar; and if the floor be occasionally sprinkled with it, the air will be much improved."
—Wiley & Putnam's Emigrant's Guide, 1845

before they proceeded into the United States. With no money to buy land and resume their agricultural lifestyle, Irish immigrants eagerly took whatever jobs were offered in the construction and maintenance of public works: bridges, railroads, canals, and coal mining; many eventually joined the Union army during the Civil War.

The perils of this rush of immigrants into New York quickly became clear. Many could not find steady work of any kind. Learning upon their arrival that the streets of New York were not paved with gold after all, most immigrants were forced into living conditions in the poorest neighborhoods. Landowners tore down the original two-story

"The chief objections to the old-style tenements are contracted quarters, lack of family privacy, and promiscuous toilet arrangements, inviting moral deterioration; lack of light and air, and of sanitary accommodations, insuring (sic) a large death rate, and danger from fire — that ever-present tenement horror. All of these are wickedly cruel when such houses are new; when they become old, dilapidated, infested with vermin and infected with disease germs, they are a disgrace to humanity and a menace, not only to the health of the unfortunate residents therein, but to the health of the whole community."
—**Editorial in *The New York Times,*** November 29, 1896

buildings that stood in the Lower East Side and replaced them with tall tenements, some up to seven stories high—long before the invention of the elevator. Forced to take odd jobs or temporary work in the hope of eventually making a decent living, thousands of immigrants lived in the city's dangerous and historically notorious slums, forming violent gangs and battling each other in the streets for control of city blocks.

Five Points—named for the five-pointed star created by the intersection of what are now Worth, Little Water, Baxter, and Mulberry Streets—became one of New York City's greatest embarrassments, a pit of destitution and squalid living conditions where people lived eight or ten to a room. Here disease ran rampant, spread by the utter lack of sanitation and wastes that mixed with the only water source. With no running water and a lack of any kind of sanitary convenience, tenants were forced to use a community pit as a toilet, making dysentery the most common illness throughout the tenements—closely followed by typhus, cholera, and tuberculosis. Infants born into this misery had only a 20 percent chance of survival.

Not surprisingly, Five Points and the cluster of tenements in an area called the Bend rapidly became Manhattan's most dangerous slums, hotbeds for clashes between Irish, Italians, and native-born Americans. Crime became a way of life born of desperation, and so many Irish immigrants were arrested for a myriad of infractions that the police referred to their vans as "paddy wagons," a reference to the common Irish nickname for Patrick.

By the mid-1850s, there were more Irish-born immigrants in New York City than in any city in the

Five Points became the world's most notorious slum.

country. Recognizing the strength of such a massive population from one country, the men who ran Tammany Hall reached out to these immigrants, making them the engine that drove the political machine that would shape the city, for better or worse, for the next eighty years. In return, Tammany Hall worked to find jobs for the city's poorest residents, provided them with food, coal, and other necessities in times of greatest need, and even paid the rent for destitute families who had fallen on the hardest of times. All of this humanitarian assistance bought the loyalty of a grateful population, pushing this immigrant-friendly machine into the forefront of New York City politics.

"Around 'the Bend' cluster the bulk of the tenements that are stamped together as altogether bad, even by the optimists of the Health Department. Incessant raids cannot keep down the crowds that make them their home. In the scores of back alleys, of stable lanes and hidden byways, of which the rent collector alone can keep track, they share such shelter as the ramshackle structures afford with every kind of abomination rifled from the dumps and ash barrels of the city. Here, too, shunning the light, skulks the unclean beast of dishonest idleness."
—**Jacob Riis**

The transition from abject poverty to a healthy existence took time, and required the help of everyone in the family to boost the household income. Women served as domestic staff to the wealthy and as teachers in New York City schools. Men built bridges, roads, and buildings, or moved out of the city to take jobs in the construction of the Erie Canal, work in Pennsylvania's coal mines, or lay tracks for the transcontinental railroad.

When the Civil War began and Union officials came through to recruit men into the army, many chose service to their new country as a reasonable alternative to the hard labor they endured in construction. These men formed some of the most celebrated ranks of the Union's forces: The Irish Brigade—the "Fighting 69th" of the New York Infantry—played a significant role in the first and second battles of Manassas, as well as in the trenches at Antietam, the storming of Marye's Heights at Fredericksburg, and the Wheatfield at

General Robert Nugent and officers of New York's Irish Brigade led an immigrant force into the Civil War.

Gettysburg. More than half of its ranks did not return from the war.

Women and children left to fend for themselves by the absence, death, or disappearance of husbands and fathers had few options open to them. Despite considerable efforts, Tammany Hall could not rescue everyone from the misery and shame of insolvency, and the only social service program offered by the city was Outdoor Relief, through which the government provided bread and coal to the poorest families. Those who reached the bottom of their resources might end up in the poorhouse on Randall's Island (well uptown, in the East River). To survive, women took in piecework, sometimes with the help of their older children.

The power of the Tammany Society would undergo considerable expansion in 1870, however, as William M. "Boss" Tweed, a former grand sachem of Tammany Hall, became New York City's commissioner of public works. The scandal that followed would change the way Tammany Hall did business for more than a decade to come.

Eastern Europeans Move West

In 1848, revolutions swept across Europe in an attempt to form a democratic government in Germany and throughout the Austro-Hungarian Empire. When these revolutions failed, the people who supported this fight for human rights found themselves on the governments' most-wanted lists, leaving them no choice but to vacate their native lands. This fairly elite group, known as the "Forty-Eighters," fled from Germany, Czechoslovakia, and Hungary to Canada, Australia, and

Carl Schurz was one of the "Forty-Eighters," and a major-general in the Civil War.

the United States, and for these men and their families, the immigration story turned out to be very different from those who arrived poor and desperate. The Forty-Eighters were generally well educated, and they brought with them the wealth they had accumulated through their work in their homelands, as well as their strong sense of the need for human rights, democratic government, and fundamental freedoms for all citizens. Many became dedicated crusaders against slavery and nativism, a new movement in the United States that fostered prejudice by native-born Americans against the immigrants arriving in America's ports.

Thousands of Forty-Eighters enlisted in the Union army when the Civil War began, and some became Civil War generals: Carl Schurz, Alexander Schimmelpfennig, and Louis Blenker are all familiar names to historians and Civil War buffs today. Others continued their work as writers, journalists, musicians, political activists, and leaders in industry, the most notable of whom was Joseph Spiegel, a German Forty-Eighter and founder of the Spiegel Catalog.

A Pass-through for the Chinese

While the Germans, Austrians, Czechs, and Hungarians fled eastern Europe in 1848 to escape persecution by their home governments, the first Chinese immigrants began to arrive in California. Spurred by news of the Gold Rush on America's west coast, they left a homeland where flood and famine had robbed them of their ability to make a living, to seek their fortunes in the wild, pre-statehood territories across the Pacific Ocean.

By the early 1850s, as a revolution began in China and social upheaval destroyed the last opportunities to support their families, the Chinese began to arrive in California in significant numbers—as many as 300,000 between 1851 and 1864. As gold fever began to wane, however, and the yields turned out to be smaller than anticipated, the Chinese moved on to construction jobs on the Central Railroad, becoming the nation's greatest source of labor as the tracks extended eastward. In 1868, in the interest of normalizing relations between the United States and China, the two countries ratified the Burlingame-Seward Treaty, which allowed Chinese and United States citizens to emigrate freely from one country to the other.

The following year, on May 10, 1869, some 12,000 Chinese immigrants completed the western half of the transcontinental railroad, fulfilling the task they were recruited to complete. What the government had not taken into account, however, was that many of these immigrants expected to stay in America, where they had steady work and reasonable wages that allowed them to support their families in California or back home in China. With the railroad completed, the Chinese moved into other jobs usually held by white laborers— in cigar rolling and textiles, on a levee project in the Sacramento–San Joaquin River Delta, and as migrant farm workers. They were ready to accept lower pay than their white counterparts, a strategy that brought them into direct conflict with natural-born Americans, who believed they were losing jobs to these immigrants. Waves of violence soon drove the Chinese out of these jobs, and they began to move east.

Begin your tour at the Lower East Side Tenement Museum, in the heart of New York's original immigration district.

Tour the restored tenement at 97 Orchard Street during your visit to the Lower East Side Tenement Museum.

1. Lower East Side Tenement Museum. The meticulously restored tenement building at 97 Orchard Street—one of the only remaining tenements from the 1800s—housed 120 people at a time in just a handful of apartments, for a total of 7,000 residents over its seventy-two-year life span. Rescued from demolition by historians Ruth Abram and Anita Jacobson in 1988, the building now offers the most realistic view we've found of immigrants' lives from the 1860s until 1935. Take a tour and learn about the families who lived in this tenement, and see the cramped, gritty conditions in which they raised families, eked out their living, and became part of the American fabric. Guided tours each feature a single floor of the tenement building, and last about an hour. 108 Orchard St., (212) 982-8420, www.tenement.org. Museum daily 10:15–5. Museum shop daily 10–6. Closed Thanksgiving, Christmas, and New Year's Day. Advance ticket purchase strongly recommended. $17–$22. LOWER EAST SIDE

2. Beth Hamedrash Hagadol. Originally the Norfolk Street Baptist Church when it was constructed in 1852, this Gothic Revival building now houses the oldest Russian Jewish congregation in the United States. The congregation Beth Hamedrash Hagadol, also founded in 1852, purchased the building in 1885. Among more than a century of leaders was Jacob Joseph, who became New York City's chief rabbi in the early 1900s—the only rabbi

Beth Hamedrash Hagadol housed the oldest Jewish congregation in the U.S.

ever to hold this short-lived title. 60–64 Norfolk Street, (212) 374-4100, www.nyc-architecture.com/LES/LES014.htm. By appointment only. Donations appreciated. LOWER EAST SIDE

3. St. Mary's Church. Founded by Irish immigrants, the third Catholic church in New York moved to this location from Sheriff Street after a fire set by nativist vandals in 1831 nearly destroyed the original building. The congregation laid the cornerstone for this building in 1832, and began holding services here in June 1833. The Romanesque façade you see here was added in 1864 by designer Patrick C. Keely, replacing the Greek

You are welcome to step inside the elegant sanctuary of St. Mary's Church.

Revival structure that fronted the church for its first 32 years. Today the church is still staffed by Irish-Americans, while the congregation has shifted to a Latino base. 440 Grand Street, at Ridge Street, www.saintmarysles.org. Open for mass and prayer daily 9–5. Free. LOWER EAST SIDE

4. Bialystoker Synagogue. Founded by Jews who arrived from the town of Bialystok in Poland, this Orthodox Jewish synagogue was first organized in 1865 as the Chevra Anshei Chesed of Bialystok. The congregation began in a building on Hester Street, then moved to Orchard Street and ultimately to its present location, the former Willet Street Methodist Episcopal Church—a late-Federal-style fieldstone building constructed in 1826. Call ahead to arrange for a tour, which includes the striking interior—added during the Great Depression to serve as an inspiration to the afflicted community—and a break in the wall in a corner of the women's gallery (balcony seating in

Built in 1826 as a Methodist church, Bialystoker Synagogue offers tours by appointment.

the sanctuary) leading to an attic that served as a hideaway for escaped slaves on the Underground Railroad. 7–11 Willett Street/Bialystoker Place, (212) 475-0165, www.bialystoker.org. Call for a tour (best times are Mon–Fri 7–10 a.m.). Donations appreciated. LOWER EAST SIDE

5. Five Points (now Columbus Park). Five streets once converged at the south end of Columbus Park, site of the first tenements constructed in the 1810s to house the influx of Irish and German immigrants. Until 1808, this was a swamp

Today, children play where gangs once battled over territory in Five Points.

with some tanneries skirting its edges; the city chose to fill in this area and build Pearl Street over the fragile land. Not surprisingly, in a few years the street began to sink into the unstable land beneath it, and a terrible smell of swamp gas and decay emanated from the earth. Those who could afford to live elsewhere rapidly vacated, leaving the miserable area to the poor. By the 1840s, Five Points was one of the world's worst and most dangerous slums. Jacob Riis, author of *How the Other Half Lives,* referred to this area as "a foul corner of New York's slums," and devoted an entire chapter of the book to photographs revealing the squalor in the area. Today it's a pleasant park with playgrounds for neighborhood children (though you should skip using the not-so-pleasant public restrooms here). The lengthening and shortening of the original

Abraham Florentine: At the Center of the Crucible

Here at what is now Columbus Park, the home of Abraham Florentine stood at 59½ Mulberry Street. Florentine, a thirty-year-old undertaker, was one of only a handful of native-born Americans living in the Bend slums in 1855, and his very presence was an issue for the thousands of Irish and Italian immigrants who reluctantly called Five Points their home. The young Florentine had been listed as a candidate on the Sixth-Ward Reform ticket for one of three city council seats, aligning him with the nativist group the Five Pointers called the Know Nothings. The nativists were native-born Americans who looked down on the immigrants as ignorant, inferior, and a burden to the nation.

When Florentine was hired by the Metropolitan Police Force, the gang leadership in the neighborhood took this as a sign that the police were making a drastic change in the force—away from the mostly Irish immigrants who protected the streets, and toward the nativists. This conflict came to a head on July 4, 1857, when Florentine was attacked in the street. The assault became the catalyst for a riot between the Bowery Boys, who supported the police, and a pro-immigrant gang known as the Roche Guard—or the Dead Rabbits by those who opposed it. Walter Roche, an Irish saloon owner with deep political connections, sponsored the Roche Guard.

As the conflict escalated, rocks and brickbats quickly gave way to knives and guns, and casualties began to mount as the police worked to quell the fighting. Despite their efforts, seven people were dead by the end of the night, and thirty-nine more were taken to hospitals or to their homes with serious injuries. Final reports by *The New York Times* raised the casualty figures to eight dead, forty-three injured, while smaller riots broke out at 487 Eighth Avenue and at the corner of 23rd Street, landing more gang members in jail. Florentine himself survived the attack and the subsequent riot, ducking into a bar that was known to be a Bowery Boys stronghold.

The Bowery Boys and Dead Rabbits clash at Five Points.

streets ended their convergence here, so only Worth and Baxter Streets still form the remaining "point." CHINATOWN

6. A. T. Stewart and Company. The "cradle of the department store," A. T. Stewart was the first major store of its kind to sell a wide range of dry goods. From its meager beginnings as a one-room shop, A. T. Stewart grew to become the largest store in the world at the time of its construction. This "Marble Palace," as it was known in the industry because of its slick marble facade, made Scots/Irish immigrant Alexander T. Stewart one of the richest men in New York. 280 Broadway, at the corner of Chambers Street (now a New York City municipal office building). Not open to the public. CITY HALL

". . . You will deal with ignorant, opinionated and innocent people. You will often have an opportunity to cheat them. If they could, they would cheat you, or force you to sell at less than cost. You must be wise, but not too wise. You must never actually cheat the customer, even if you can. . . . You must make her happy and satisfied, so she will come back."
—Alexander T. Stewart

7. St. Patrick's Old Cathedral. Dedicated in 1815, this was the first cathedral in the newly created Roman Catholic Diocese of New York City. It was enlarged in 1838–42, then nearly met its end when mob violence threatened—the Ancient Order of Hibernians, an Irish Catholic fraternity, defended the cathedral with muskets and barricades when the Know Nothing mob attacked and attempted to burn St. Patrick's to the ground. Twenty-two years later, in 1866, a fire nearly destroyed the cathedral. The reconstructed cathedral was rededicated in 1868; this stunning Gothic sanctuary is what we see today. In 1879, when the new St. Patrick's Cathedral opened uptown, this one became a parish church. 260–264 Mulberry Street, between Prince and Mott Streets; rectory at 263 Mulberry Street. (212) 226-8075, www.oldcathedral.org.

Old St. Patrick's was the first
cathedral of the newly formed
Diocese of New York.

Rectory Mon–Fri 8–5; mass Mon–Fri at 9 a.m. and
12:10 p.m., Fri at 7:30 p.m., Sat at 9 a.m., Sun at
9:15 and 12:45; vigil Sat at 5:30 p.m. LITTLE ITALY

8. Grace Church. This Episcopal church is easily
mistaken for the much larger St. Patrick's Cathedral, because the same architect—James Renwick—was responsible for both churches' ornate
Gothic Revival design. The congregation formed
in 1808 and built this impressive edifice from 1843
to 1846, adding its most striking marble spire in
1883 to replace a wooden tower. During the height
of immigration, the church's congregation played
a significant role in supporting the poorest immigrants, providing food and social services to as
many people as possible. The site that now holds
the church's extensive gardens once housed the
famous Fleischmann's Vienna Bakery, where the
proprietor gave away hundreds of loaves of unsold
bread daily to the poor—creating the original
"bread line." 802 Broadway, at 10th Street, (212)
254-2000, www.gracechurchnyc.org. Daily 12–5;
services Wed 6 p.m., and Sun 9, 11 and 6 p.m.
Donations appreciated. DOWNTOWN

Architect James Renwick designed Grace Church, a stunning
example of Gothic Revival style.

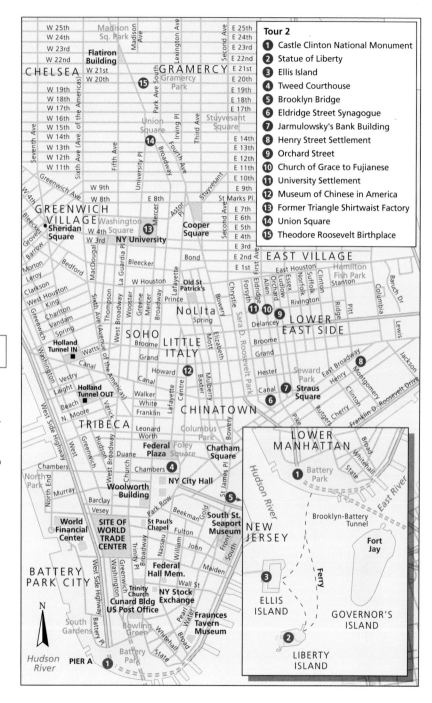

New York Immigrant Experience

Tour 2

1. Castle Clinton National Monument
2. Statue of Liberty
3. Ellis Island
4. Tweed Courthouse
5. Brooklyn Bridge
6. Eldridge Street Synagogue
7. Jarmulowsky's Bank Building
8. Henry Street Settlement
9. Orchard Street
10. Church of Grace to Fujianese
11. University Settlement
12. Museum of Chinese in America
13. Former Triangle Shirtwaist Factory
14. Union Square
15. Theodore Roosevelt Birthplace

Tour 2: 1871–1920

Politics, Prejudice, and Long Overdue Reform

With the end of the Civil War came the return of Irish immigrants to New York City, swelling the population to its prewar level and tipping the scales of power in their favor. By the late 1860s, more than a quarter of the city's population had been born in Ireland—more than enough to support candidates for political office.

This was the environment in which William M. "Boss" Tweed, formerly the Grand Sachem of Tammany Hall, was elected handily to the New York State Senate in 1867. Three years later, he left the senate to become New York City's commissioner of public works in 1870.

Tweed assembled a political machine that hid one of the most extensive embezzlement schemes in American history, bilking taxpayers out of somewhere between $40 and $200 million—an astonishing sum in 1870s dollars. His methods were remarkably simple: He and his cronies multiplied each invoice to the city by as much as 100 times,

Tammany Hall, decorated for the 1868 Democratic Convention.

Tammany's "four knaves": Tweed, Hall, Sweeny and Connolly.

New York Immigrant Experience

and he split the difference between himself and Mayor A. Oakley Hall, Park Commissioner Peter Barr Sweeny, and Richard B. Connolly, controller of public expenditures.

The simplicity of Tweed's crimes did not make them easy to track, however, especially in a world in which records were handwritten and invoices could easily slide away into obscurity. It took the combined efforts of city sheriff James O'Brien, future New York mayor William H. Wickham, and Samuel J. Tilden, who would later run for president, to reign in the rampant scheme and bring the embezzler to justice. Boss Tweed was convicted of his crimes in 1873, but a higher court shortened his sentence to a single year, and he was released in 1874—only to be brought up on civil charges and found guilty once again. Languishing in a debtors' prison, Tweed managed to escape and made for the open sea on a Spanish ship . . . where the Spanish government caught up with him and turned him over to American authorities. In 1878, Tweed died in the Ludlow Street Jail.

It's a testament to the power of Tammany Hall that the robust political machine survived this string of crimes committed by one of its most prominent leaders. Notably, the organization's power endured into the 1930s, long after this scandal had left the front pages of the daily papers. In 1874, Tammany Hall would help elect Wickham as mayor in a stunning piece of political strategy—backing the man who had personally taken down Boss Tweed—while the Irish maintained their significant role in New York's expanding Roman Catholic Church, the New York City Fire Department, and the Police Department.

Richard Croker

In 1890, Richard Croker became the leader of Tammany Hall, orchestrating the election of Robert A. Van Wyck as the first mayor of the five-borough New York City and, according to historians, controlling the city's politics through him. Croker was known to take bribes from the city's saloons, gambling dens, and prostitution rings, but he somehow retained power despite the attacks on his character. He resigned in 1901 after failing to get his candidate, Edward Shepard, elected as mayor. The greatest achievements of Tammany Hall were still to come, however, as the organization worked to choose and support a candidate for president of the United States.

New York's Complexion Changes

In the years after the Civil War through the end of the nineteenth century, New York's ethnic mix began to change once again as people looked westward from Europe and eastward from Asia toward the growth and prosperity they imagined in America. Italians began to arrive in great numbers, culminating in the highest total immigration of any single nation: Between 1876 and 1976, more than 4.5 million Italians made the crossing to the United States. Most came from southern Italy—Naples, Calabria, or Sicily—to escape rampant poverty and a series of natural disasters that afflicted the country's rural southern areas. Today, Italians remain the largest group of immigrants to have come to the United States.

In New York, Italians became fishermen, shoemakers, fruit sellers, and waiters. Many others took on day-labor jobs in construction and

"Their methods were curiously simple and primitive. There were no skilful manipulations of figures, making detection difficult. . . . Men with claims against the city—Ring favorites, most of them—were told to multiply the amount of each bill by five, or ten, or a hundred, after which, with Mayor Hall's 'O. K.' and Connolly's indorsement (sic), it was paid without question. The money was not handed to the claimant, direct, but paid through a go-between, who cashed the check, settled the original bill and divided the reminder . . . between Tweed, Sweeny, Connolly and Hall—Tweed and Connolly getting twenty-five percent, each, and Sweeny, Hall and the underlings the residue."
—Albert Bigelow Paine, historian

Italian and Irish immigrants built Brooklyn Bridge—often at great personal risk.

mining, showing a marked willingness to work for low wages and to scrimp on food to save money. Italians weren't afraid to do the tough jobs, taking whatever positions were available and working to build a new infrastructure for New York—building the Brooklyn Bridge, digging sewers and tunnels, and handling some of the dangerous work of constructing the tallest buildings in the world. By 1890, Italians had usurped many of the jobs that had been held by the Irish, creating rivalries between men of the two countries for the most desirable construction jobs. By the mid-1910s, Italians had become the dominant laborers in the garment industry, replacing the Jews who had taken these sweatshop jobs upon their arrival in New York.

When immigrant labor completed the construction of elevated transit to Harlem, well north of Five Points and the tenements in which most immigrants still lived, the new neighborhood attracted German, Irish, Italian, Lebanese, and Russian immigrants to look north for work and a better place to live. An Italian Harlem emerged, filling quickly as southern Italians and Sicilians chose East Harlem as their new place of residence. Generally, however, Italians did not make New York City their cultural center. Most Italians came from farming communities, bringing skills with them that could only be applied to the agricultural life they knew, so many moved on to areas where they could continue in the farming life. Italian immigration was heavily male, with few dependants making the difficult Atlantic crossing, so these men were particularly mobile and could go to wherever work presented itself. Many moved to upstate

New York's agricultural areas and beyond, settling in Rochester, Buffalo, and parts west. In the end, about a third of Italian immigrants eventually returned to Italy with money in hand to lift their families out of the poverty they endured at home.

A handful of high-profile Italians chose lives of crime, committing acts so notorious that their names are still household words: in particular, Al Capone and Lucky Luciano were two of the most famous criminals in American history. The U.S. Department of Justice estimates that less than 0.0025 percent of Italian-Americans are involved in organized crime, however, and Italians make up only a tiny fraction of incarcerated criminals. While John Gotti Jr. (see page 12) and the Gambino, Genovese, Bonanno, and Colombo families perpetuated the stereotype with their own heinous acts into the 1990s, the heyday of mob-related crime sweeping through New York appears to be in the past, ending with the conviction of Gotti in April 1992.

Asian Immigrants: Targets of Early Discrimination

While the greatest number of Chinese immigrants chose the California coast for their entry into the United States, the impact of their arrival resonated across the country. White Americans who moved to the new western states in pursuit of job opportunities suddenly found themselves without the work they sought, in part because of the influx of Chinese and Japanese workers who were willing to work for less money than their American counterparts— leaving natural-born Americans scrambling to find the work these perceived interlopers could not fill.

HARPER'S WEEKLY
JOURNAL OF CIVILIZATION

Most Chinese immigrants
entered the country through
California.

In consternation, citizens complained to their Congressional representatives, and their elected officials took action. First came the Page Act in 1875, which forbade all Asian women who were considered "obnoxious" by U.S. consulate representatives at their point of departure to embark to the States. The act was meant to discourage prostitutes from entering the country, but it actually prohibited many honest women as well, greatly reducing opportunities for Asian women to come to this country. The result was a lopsided ratio of Chinese and Japanese men to women in America, making it exceedingly difficult for the men, who were left with the choice to sail without their families or to remain in their home country.

In search of a more hospitable environment than California, where lawmakers passed a pile of legislation aimed at driving the Chinese out, the Asian immigrants began to cross the continent to New York City. The first Chinese grocery opened its doors on Mott Street in 1878. That same year, in a landmark decision, a federal district court in California ruled that Chinese people were not eligible for naturalized citizenship.

By the early 1880s, between 200 and 1,100 Chinese had moved into Five Points. Some of these men and women were smuggled illegally into New Jersey to work in a laundry, and moved on to New York when they could free themselves from this involuntary servitude. Once they found their way to the burgeoning Asian nucleus in the big city, these immigrants opened hand laundries all over town, supporting themselves through their own ingenuity while creating a self-sufficient community, one that did not require the assistance of

Chinese immigrants began to arrive on Mott Street in the 1880s.

outside politicians, law enforcement, or charitable aid. The new neighborhood on the outskirts of Five Points became known as Chinatown, a community with its own social services, jobs, associations, and infrastructure. As more Chinese immigrants arrived in New York, the town-within-a-city continued to support the newcomers by finding them living arrangements and jobs.

In 1882, Congress passed the Chinese Exclusion Act, prohibiting Chinese citizens from entering the United States for ten years and making the Chinese the first nationality to be denied free immigration. The Geary Act of 1892 extended the Chinese Exclusion Act for another ten years, adding the requirement that all Chinese residents carry a resident permit; failure to carry this permit was punishable with deportation. Chinese could not bear witness in court, and they could not receive bail. Worst of all, the act prohibited women and children from joining their husbands and fathers in America. At the turn of the century, the government estimated that only between 40 and 150 women lived in New York's Chinatown, in contrast to the 7,000 Chinese men there. As the law forbade Chinese men to marry white women, the unnatural imbalance led to rumors of opium dens, slave girls, and prostitution in the Chinese community.

A glimmer of hope for the Chinese living in America came in 1898, when a landmark decision by U.S. Supreme Court determined that Wong Kim Ark, a natural-born American of Chinese descent, was indeed a U.S. citizen and should be readmitted into the United States. Those hopes were dashed once again in 1904, however, when Congress voted to make the Chinese Exclusion Acts indefinite. Within days, law enforcement officials arrested 250 Chinese immigrants without producing search warrants, alleging that these residents were in the country illegally.

A Bigger, Better Registration Center

When Samuel Ellis, a private citizen, sold his island to the federal government in 1808, he parted with his property because he saw its use as a strategic location for New York City's military defense. Indeed, Ellis Island's first government use was as the site of Fort Gibson, part of the harbor's defense system that included Castle Clinton at Battery Park, Castle Williams on Governor's Island, Fort Wood on Bedloe's Island, and two earthen forts at the Verrazano Narrows.

Once the United States began building forts to withstand the more destructive firepower of nineteenth-century weapons, however, Fort Gibson was dismantled to make way for a naval magazine for munitions storage. What better place

Ellis Island became New York's immigration center in 1892.

to position a gateway to American immigration, then, than on this island in New York Harbor? Its location could not be more appropriate: at the gateway to the nation's largest city, and just across the water from the Statue of Liberty—a sparkling gift received from France in 1886, and a welcoming symbol to the world's downtrodden as they arrived on the nation's edge.

Ellis Island became the number-one destination for immigrants from all over Europe and Asia over the course of 52 years, from 1892 until 1954. More than twelve million immigrants entered the country through Ellis Island—depositing their luggage in the main building's great hall, making their way through a brief but critical medical examination, and proceeding upstairs to the Registration Room to endure questioning before their release into their new homeland.

The Floodgates Open

From the 1890s through 1930, Ellis Island saw as many as 5,000 immigrants a day come through its doors to enter the United States. Steam power made the crossing much shorter and the conditions a little easier to bear, attracting the poor and persecuted from countries throughout the Middle East, the Mediterranean, and southern and eastern Europe.

The largest populations came from nations in the thick of political strife: Four million came from the Austro-Hungarian Empire, while 3.3 million left Russia for America and 2.8 million abandoned their homes in Germany. England saw 2.3 million people board ships for North America, while 1.1 million Swedes bought overseas passage and entered the United States. Some 450,000 Greek immigrants came to escape the Ottoman rule, the Balkan Wars, and World War I, all of which had brought military conflict to their own doorsteps. Most of the early Greek immigration was male, and they took

Five thousand immigrants a day passed through Ellis Island.

> *"Give me your tired, your poor,*
> *Your huddled masses yearning to breathe free,*
> *The wretched refuse of your teeming shore.*
> *Send these, the homeless, tempest-tossed to me.*
> *I lift my lamp beside the golden door."*
> —**Inscription at the base of the Statue of Liberty, written by Emma Lazarus**

Immigrants brought all that they could carry from their homeland in a trunk or two.

jobs in industry; some created a niche for themselves in the fur industry.

While we know that Polish immigrants arrived in great numbers in the 1890s, the actual number—estimated at 2.6 million—has proven to be tough to calculate. At the time, Poland suffered from fragmentation caused by its partition among several ruling countries, which continued through 1918. As a result, many Poles were classified as German, Russian, or Austrian in ships' manifests written at the ports from which they departed Europe. The Poles came to escape racist persecution and unemployment—a sad result of the

Most immigrants could afford only steerage tickets for the ocean crossing.

industrial revolution that usurped farmland for homes and factories. Polish farmers, devoted to their land and crops for many generations, suddenly were forced to become laborers and migrant workers—and word of America's vast open land resonated with their desire to continue the work they knew so well. When the Russian Revolution caused even greater strife in the Russian Partition of Poland, even laborers who had found industrial jobs chose to exit en masse.

The Poles sold everything they had to afford the crossing to America, arriving in New York ready to start a new life with a clean slate. Many came to make money with an eye toward returning to Poland, and their countrymen nicknamed them *za chlebem,* or "for bread" immigrants. While some did find their way to the open farmland they sought, others were recruited to the Pennsylvania coal mines and to Chicago, Pittsburgh, Detroit, Buffalo, Milwaukee, and Cleveland to work in heavy industries. Soon the midwestern steel mills, slaughterhouses, and iron and sugar refineries were packed with Polish workers.

The World's Third-Largest Jewish Community

When anti-Jewish uprisings known as pogroms drove Jews out of the Russian Empire from 1881 to 1884, the Jews exited a region called the Pale of Settlement—now Poland, Lithuania, Belarus, Ukraine, and Moldova—and sought religious freedom in the United States.

The mass exodus shifted the balance of Jewish life across the ocean and onto a new continent. In 1880, six million of the world's 7.7 million Jews lived in eastern Europe; by 1920, nearly 23 percent of the world's Jews lived in America. Most were driven to the States by the 1905 revolution in Poland, which spurred a significant wave of anti-Semitism during the rise of the country's National Democratic Party. Jewish doctors, lawyers, and merchants fled Poland as their clientele disappeared in a storm of anti-Jewish sentiment that rose to a fever pitch fueled by the Party.

Between 1890 and 1924, more than two million Jews arrived in New York. Most spoke Yiddish, which allowed them to communicate with Jews from other regions as they settled in New York City. Eager to assimilate into American life and culture, they built many small temples and *landsman-schaftn* for Jews from the same town or village, supporting one another as they had longed to do in Russia and the Pale. By 1900, the United States had 1.5 million Jewish residents, which ranked as the third-largest Jewish population in the world.

Once they were in this country, the Jews had an easier time than some of the other groups of immigrants who arrived as laborers and farmers. Most came from industrial professions and from cities, and arrived with high literacy rates and marketable skills that allowed them to become business owners, hiring their countrymen as employees. New York City became the center of Jewish life in America, with entire districts still dominated by Jewish citizens today—although most have moved out to the suburbs and beyond New York City and its environs.

Flickers of Reform at Last

It took a man of the upper class to move the City of New York to do something about the conditions tenement dwellers faced on a daily basis. Believing that "bad tenement house conditions were the cause of most of the problems in our modern cities," as he wrote in his communications with city officials, Lawrence Veiller led a movement to make sweeping changes in existing buildings and set stringent requirements for new construction.

The result was the 1901 Tenement House Act, which insisted that tenements have running water, tub sinks, and more windows for better ventilation to combat the coal-burning stoves and gas lamps that caused respiratory problems for many tenants. Tenement houses had to have indoor plumbing—specifically water closets—and the communal sinks that stood in tenement yards were removed in compliance with the law. The

The miseries of tenement life finally began to shift in 1901.

New York State Tenement House Commission, the governing body established by Governor Theodore Roosevelt in 1900, surveyed conditions in the city's tenements and made sure the new laws were implemented to the letter. Veiller became the Commission's first secretary, appointed to the post by the governor, and soon the crusader-turned-bureaucrat found himself swamped with requests for information from cities all over the country that sought to make substantive changes to their housing situations. By 1910, eleven states and forty cities had followed New York's example, adopting housing codes that began a nationwide cleanup of unlivable tenements.

Begin your tour at Battery Park, with a trip to the Statue of Liberty and Ellis Island.

1. Castle Clinton National Monument. Formerly Castle Garden, this 1811 fort once served as part of the defensive system against potential British invasion of New York City. From 1855 through 1890, it became the receiving center for hundreds of thousands of immigrants, before the registration was transferred to Ellis Island. Today it serves as the ticket office and embarkation point for ferry service to the Statue of Liberty and Ellis Island, with interpretive displays about the building's colorful history as a restaurant, theater, opera house, and the location of the New York City Aquarium. Battery Park, (212) 344-7220, www.nps.gov/cacl and www.castlegarden.org. Daily 8:30–5; closed Christmas Day. Free. BATTERY PARK

Castle Clinton—formerly Castle Garden—served as New York's first immigration receiving center.

Liberty's crown was reopened to visitors in 2009.

2. The Statue of Liberty. The most recognizable symbol of democracy and freedom in the world, the Statue came to the United States in 1886 as a gift from France, and it continues to be considered a marvel of engineering and artistic merit. Visitors can enter the museum at the Statue's base and look up through a glass ceiling to see nearly all of its 305-foot height from the inside. On July 4, 2009, the National Park Service reopened the stairway to the Statue's crown—a 354-step climb to the top—for the first time since its closure on September 11, 2001, as a security measure. Liberty Island, (212) 363-3200, www.nps.gov/stli. Daily 9:30–5; closed Christmas. Admission is free with a ferry ticket (see next page).

3. Ellis Island. Twelve million immigrants entered the United States through this registration and investigation point between 1892 and 1954. The

Planning Your Visit to the Statue of Liberty and Ellis Island

Castle Clinton is the gateway to two of the most visited sites in New York: the Statue of Liberty on Liberty Island, and the immigrant receiving center at Ellis Island. Here are the facts you need to know to maximize your enjoyment of these two national landmarks.

You must take the ferry to visit either or both sites. Ferry tickets are available at the ticket windows in Castle Clinton, or in advance at (877) LADY-TIX (523-9849) or www.statuecruises.com. The tickets can be used anytime during the day for which they have been purchased, but you must depart before 2 p.m. to visit both the Statue of Liberty and Ellis Island. From spring break until school begins after Labor Day, lines can be long for the ferry at Battery Park and on both islands; you may wait an hour or more to board a ferry. In these seasons, plan an all-day excursion to see both Liberty and Ellis Islands, and wear comfortable shoes for standing in lines.

There are four different kinds of tickets for your visit to Liberty and Ellis Islands, but all four are the same price: $12 for adults, $10 for seniors 62 and over, and $5 for children. Add the audio tour of both the Statue of Liberty and Ellis Island for a total of $20 for adults, $17.25 for seniors, and $12.25 for children (the price includes the ferry ticket):

- Buy a **Reserve Ticket** to visit Liberty Island and Ellis Island without entering the Statue. The Reserve Ticket gives you access to the restaurant, gift shop, and National Park Information Station on Liberty Island, and to all of the public areas at Ellis Island.
- Buy a **Reserve Pedestal/Museum Ticket** to enter the museum at the base of the Statue and the Pedestal Observation Deck. This includes everything but the climb

to the crown. You may wait in line to visit the museum. You will have priority access to the security screening facility before you board the ferry, which reduces your wait time. You'll go through a second security screening before you enter the Statue.

- Buy a **Reserve Crown Ticket** to make the 354-step climb to Liberty's crown. The climb is up a narrow stairway with no ventilation, so it's usually 20 degrees hotter than outside—and the National Park Service cautions that this climb is not recommended if you have heart or respiratory issues, claustrophobia, fear of heights, or vertigo. Be honest with yourself before attempting this climb. Still want to go? You'll need to buy your tickets weeks in advance, especially for weekends, holiday weeks, and summer.

- Buy a **3-day Flex Ticket,** good for one-time use during a three-day period. The Flex Ticket can only be purchased for ground access to the Statue of Liberty and Ellis Island; it does not give you access to the statue's pedestal or crown.

You will pass through airport-style federal security before boarding the ferry at Battery Park. Leave your pocketknife, tools, firearms, rolling luggage, and parcels in your car or hotel room—none will be allowed on the ferry or on the islands.

If this sounds unusually strict for a tourist attraction, consider that you are visiting one of the nation's most treasured landmarks, and that you are doing so in New York City. As you entered Battery Park, you passed the Sphere, a badly damaged sculpture that stood in the plaza of the World Trade Center for thirty years, and was rescued from the rubble during the massive excavation that followed the terrorist attacks of September 11, 2001. This is a reminder to all of us to respect and cooperate with the additional security required here.

tour begins in the Baggage Room, where immigrants left their luggage while they went through the medical inspection and questioning in the Registry Room. The main building offers an extensive museum of immigration history, with interactive exhibits that allow you to test your knowledge of American government with the questions immigrants must answer to qualify for citizenship.

Ellis Island offers several ways to make the most of your visit:

- **Wander on your own.** The materials and displays are well interpreted; there is plenty to see if you prefer independent exploration to narrated tours. Be sure to visit the third floor for information about the medical screenings and humane treatment immigrants received here.
- **Take the audio tour.** Purchase the audio tour with your ferry ticket, and pick up the headset as you enter the building. Stops on the tour are numbered in the printed museum guide you receive with your headset.
- **Take a ranger-led tour.** The free tours are 45 minutes long, and provide a solid overview of the immigration experience.
- **See the movie *Island of Hope, Island of Tears,*** to understand the history and significance of Ellis Island and its place in history. The movie is 45 minutes and is free.
- **See the live play *Taking a Chance on America,*** in which professional actors tell the story of actor Bela Lugosi's journey to America. Lugosi was made famous by his role as Dracula in a series of 1930s films.
- Whatever you do, **plan at least two to three hours** for your visit to the island.

New York Immigrant Experience

Searching for Your Ancestors on Ellis Island: What to Expect at the American Family Immigration Center

In an effort that seems nearly superhuman, the entire database of twenty-five million immigration records—the contents of sixty-three years of ships' manifests—has been made available online by the Ellis Island Foundation. You are welcome to take advantage of this extraordinary database during your visit to the island by making an appointment when you arrive.

When you disembark from the ferry at Ellis Island and enter the building, head to your left to the American Family Immigration Center, and reserve a Search Session—a time to use a computer workstation with some guidance by Ellis Island staff members to get you started. You'll be given a time to return to the center to start your search. Bring any information you have on your ancestors: the name of the ship on which they arrived, the year they came to America, alternate spellings of their names, birth dates, age when they

Get a printed copy of the ship's manifest when you find your relatives in the Immigration Center's records.

arrived, or anything else you know. The more information you have, the more successful you will be in finding names in the database. If you find your ancestor's name, the Center will print a copy of the ship's manifest that contains the name for a nominal fee.

It's fun to search the database while you're at Ellis Island, but if you'd rather spend your time touring the museum, you can do your searching from the comfort of your own home. The same database is available at www.ellisisland.org. (If you have searched the database at home and have not found your ancestor, there is no additional information on the island.)

If your ancestor does not turn up in the database, professionals at the center may be able to provide additional ideas for finding your ancestor's entry point into the United States. Not all immigrants came through Ellis Island; there were other immigration centers in Boston, Philadelphia, New Jersey, Texas, Los Angeles, and other seaports—although Ellis Island was by far the largest.

Ellis Island historians recommend some books to help you get started in your genealogical search: *The Family Tree Guide to Finding Your Ellis Island Ancestors* by Sharon DeBartolo Cormack (Family Tree Books, 2005) and *Google Your Family Tree* by Daniel M. Lynch (FamilyLink.com Inc., 2008).

(212) 363-3200, www.nps.gov/elis. Daily 9:30–5; closed Christmas. Admission is free with a ferry ticket (see above).

When you return from the ferry trip to Liberty and Ellis Islands, walk north through Battery Park to Broadway. Continue up Broadway to the corner of Chambers Street, and turn right.

4. Tweed Courthouse (Old New York County Courthouse). One of New York's greatest nineteenth-century architectural triumphs, this courthouse stands as a lasting reminder of former Tammany Hall boss William M. Tweed, who embezzled gasp-inducing sums from the city's public works budget through its construction. It was only fitting, then, that Tweed should come to justice in this building in 1873, when he was tried and convicted in an unfinished room and

William "Boss" Tweed approved the construction of the courthouse in which he was tried and convicted.

sentenced to 12 years in prison. The building itself did not reach completion until 1881, when it became home to the New York County Supreme Court. In 1929, the City Court moved in and remained until 1961, when the courthouse became a municipal office building. Today the building serves as the headquarters of the Department of Education. 52 Chambers Street, behind City Hall, (212) 639-9675 to schedule a tour, www.nyc.gov/html/artcom/html/tours/tweed.shtml. Tours for individuals are given on Fridays at noon; a reservation is required 48 hours in advance. Free. CITY HALL

Continue on Chambers Street to Park Row, and turn right. Walk down Park Row to the Brooklyn Bridge, and turn left onto the road to the bridge.

5. Brooklyn Bridge. Designed by a German immigrant and built predominantly by men of Irish and Italian origins, this bridge is one of the city's greatest monuments to the accomplishments of America's newcomers. John Augustus Roebling designed several suspension bridges before he took on the engineering of this marvel, a project he began on his own when he became frustrated with the ferry service to and from Brooklyn. This bridge became Roebling's masterwork, requiring feats of engineering never attempted before—and the entire project nearly derailed when "caisson disease," what we now know as decompression sickness (colloquially called "the bends"), incapacitated the designer's son, project leader Washington Roebling. Today we can walk or drive the bridge's 6,016 feet and stand at its midpoint, 135 feet above the East River below. Spanning

A Guided Tour through History

Designed by a German immigrant, Brooklyn Bridge owes its construction to Irish and Italian workers.

from New York to Brooklyn via FDR Drive, Park Row, Chambers/Centre Streets, and Pearl/Frank-fort Streets. Pedestrians can access the Brooklyn side from Tillary/Adams Streets or from a staircase on Prospect Street between Cadman Plaza East and West; on the Manhattan side from the end of Centre Street or the south staircase of Brooklyn Bridge–City Hall subway station. Always open. Free. LOWER EAST SIDE

6. Museum at Eldridge Street/Eldridge Street Synagogue. Beautifully restored in 2007, this Moorish Revival temple was designed by two Roman Catholic tenement builders and opened in 1887, just in time for the Rosh Hashanah and Yom Kippur observance. The synagogue became one of the first in New York to be built specifically for Jewish worship, moving its congregation out of its makeshift space and into this distinctive temple.

Eldridge Street Synagogue tells the compelling story of its first congregation.

Congregation Kahal Adath Jeshurun continues to meet in this synagogue, and the building does double-duty as a museum, telling the stories of the first immigrants who worshiped under the sanctuary's 50-foot vaulted ceiling. 12 Eldridge Street, (212) 219-0302, www.eldridgestreet.org. By guided tour only, Sun–Thurs 10–5. Adults $10, seniors (62+) $8, children ages 5–18 $6, ages 5 and under free. LOWER EAST SIDE

7. Jarmulowsky's Bank Building. One of the tallest buildings on the Lower East Side when it was constructed in 1912, this building housed the bank founded by Sender Jarmulowsky, a Russian immigrant and ordained rabbi who arrived in New York in the early 1870s. Jarmulowsky moved to Hamburg, Germany, in 1868 and opened a passage and exchange business, coming to New York in 1873 to open a second office at the location that

Sender Jarmulowsky moved his successful bank to this building in 1912.

now bears his name. His excellent reputation for honesty led him to achieve great success—but in the panic that preceded World War I, customers withdrew their funds all at once to send overseas to help their relatives, and the bank collapsed. The building now holds offices. 54/58 Canal Street, www.lowereastsideny.com/leshistory.htm. Not open to the public. LOWER EAST SIDE

8. Henry Street Settlement. Founded in 1893 and operating continuously since then, the Henry Street Settlement was one of the first establishments to carry out the tenets of the social reform movement that emerged at the end of the nineteenth century. Desperate for relief from the miserable living conditions and rampant disease they endured, the Lower East Side residents turned to settlement houses within their neighborhoods for assistance that helped them improve their lives—health care, employment services, tutoring in English and reading, and other services for new immigrants and the poor. Today, the house serves the Asian and Latino residents of the surrounding neighborhood. Visit the Abrons Arts Center at 466

Grand Street, one of the nation's first arts facilities to provide low-income populations access to the arts. While open to the public, the settlement house has no official tours or displays; enjoy a visit to the Arts Center instead. Henry Street Settlement 263–267 Henry Street, (212) 766-9200; Abrons Art Center 466 Grand Street, (212) 598-0400; www.henrystreet.org. Arts Center gallery: Mon–Sat 9 a.m.–10 p.m., Sun 10 a.m.–6 p.m. Ticket price varies with exhibition. LOWER EAST SIDE

This settlement house continues to serve the neighborhood's residents.

9. Orchard Street. Once the center of Jewish life in New York—a street lined with pushcarts and tenements—Orchard Street continues to be a major tourist attraction as a shopping district for clothing, shoes, luggage, handbags, and more at rarely seen discount prices. Every Sunday, the street closes to vehicular traffic to create a pedestrian mall, where merchants line the sidewalks with bargains. It's no wonder that this is still one of the busiest shopping districts in the world. Look for lingerie shops and men's clothing stores below Delancey Street; from Delancey to East Houston, it's all discount clothing and luggage. For

A Guided Tour through History

Orchard Street retains its nineteenth century flavor.

the best prices, bring cash. Eight city blocks long, from Division Street in Chinatown to East Houston Street on the Lower East Side, (212) 226-9010, www.lowereastsideny.com. CHINATOWN, LOWER EAST SIDE

10. Church of Grace to Fujianese. This building now houses a church that serves Chinese Christian immigrants who come from the Fujian province, but it began as the Municipal Bath House, one of 15 free public bathhouses constructed in the early twentieth century that provided tenement

New York Immigrant Experience

Formerly a public bathhouse, this church now serves the Fujianese population.

dwellers with a place to wash in clean water. Generally, immigrants living in the surrounding slums had no bathtubs, making personal hygiene a daily challenge. The social reforms of the early 1900s led to centers like this one; when Mayor Fiorello LaGuardia ordered more sweeping housing reforms in the 1930s, these bathhouses were no longer required. 133 Allen Street, (212) 254-3886, www.cgfchurch.org. Not open to the public. LOWER EAST SIDE

11. University Settlement. University is the oldest settlement house in America, established in 1886 by a small group of reformers who "settled" into the Lower East Side community, studied its problems, and set themselves to the task of creating solutions. The founders eschewed the traditional ideas of handouts and charity, and instead worked to provide education, advice, and a break from the jarring realities that surrounded the immigrant residents. University Settlement provided the first public bath, the first kindergarten, and the concept of Head Start—giving preschoolers a foundation in learning before they started school. Today its programs continue to assist children and adults on the Lower East Side, in Chinatown, and in the East Village. 184 Eldridge Street, (212) 674-9120, www .universitysettlement.org. Not open to the public. LOWER EAST SIDE

12. Museum of Chinese in America. This brand-new museum, opened in September 2009, provides an unprecedented view of the history, culture, and experiences of people of Chinese descent in the United States. Its modern interior

The brand-new Museum of Chinese in America uses innovative interpretive styles.

is a 14,000-square-foot space with multiple exhibition galleries, interactive kiosks, and a traditional Chinese courtyard in the center, where a permanent exhibition combines video screens and original brick structural walls to portray the experiences of Chinese immigrants, many of whom became deadlocked between American and Chinese political struggles. Created by Maya Lin—the designer of the Vietnam Veterans Memorial in Washington, D.C.—the museum features the Journey Wall, covered with bronze tiles inscribed with names of immigrants and ancestors of today's Chinese-American community. 211–215 Centre Street between Howard and Grand Streets, (212) 619-4785, www.mocanyc.org. Mon and Fri 11–5, Thurs 11–9, Sat–Sun 10–5; closed Tues and Wed. Adults $7, senior citizens (65+) and students $4, children under 12 free. CHINATOWN

13. Triangle Shirtwaist Factory (now the Brown Building of Science). On March 25, 1911, in one of the worst industrial disasters in American history, a fire broke out on one of the top floors of the Triangle Shirtwaist Factory. Workers rushing to escape the blaze found the ninth floor doors locked from the outside, imprisoning them in a burning building, while the outside fire escape proved too weak to hold the frantic workers. Facing the choice between death by burning or falling, many leapt from ninth floor windows in a vain attempt to save themselves. In the end, the fire killed 146 of the 500 garment workers, most of them immigrants from Italy and eastern Europe—who already endured low wages, long hours, and unsanitary working conditions. The tragedy resulted in formation of the International Ladies' Garment Workers' Union, eventually putting an end to the sweatshops. 23–29 Washington Place (east of Washington Square Park). Not open to the public. GREENWICH VILLAGE

"The days were long and the wages low—my starting wage was just one dollar and a half a week—a long week—consisting more often than not, of seven days. Especially was this true during the season, which in those days were longer than they are now. I will never forget the sign which on Saturday afternoons was posted on the wall near the elevator stating—'if you don't come in on Sunday you need not come in on Monday'! What choice did we have except to look for another job on Monday morning. We did not relish the thought of walking the factory district in search of another job. And would we find a better one? We did not like it. As a matter of fact we looked forward to the one day on which we could sleep a little longer, go to the park and get to see one's friends and relatives. It was a bitter disappointment."
—**Pauline M. Newman, Lithuanian immigrant and Triangle Shirtwaist Factory employee**

A woman carries home heavy piecework after a day of factory work.

Union Square hosts a perpetual open-air arts market in spring and summer.

14. Union Square. Reviewing stands for the nation's first Labor Day parade stood here, while more than 10,000 workers marched past on September 5, 1882, before gathering here in what was then called Wendel's Elm Park for a picnic and concert. The sight of so many workers—a labor force that made New York City the nation's largest industrial center—certainly must have impressed the owners of the many sweatshops that produced garments and other goods throughout the city. Improvements to working conditions, however, would not come for more than two decades. Today the square serves as a gathering place where artists and craftspeople offer their work for sale in the spring and summer months. Bounded by East 14th Street, Union Square West, East 16th Street, and Park Avenue South, (212) 460-1200, www.union squarenyc.org. Always open. Free. UNION SQUARE

15. Theodore Roosevelt Birthplace National Historic Site. If you'd like to get a sense of how people lived uptown from the tenements, this Dutch-inspired brownstone and its meticulously preserved interior will open your eyes. Roosevelt, a descendant of Dutch immigrants, came into the world in a gilded existence tempered only by his chronic asthma and other childhood illnesses. His parents' elegant former home features many furnishings that remain from young Teedie's childhood, including the boy-sized red velvet chair he favored. The museum here provides a peek into the life of the man who worked to pass legislation in the New York State Assembly in the 1880s to improve tenement conditions, prior to becoming president of the United States. 28 East 20th Street, (212) 260-1616, www.nps.gov/thrb. Tues–Sat 9–5; rooms by guided tour only, at 10, 11, 1, 2, 3, and 4. Free. DOWNTOWN

Theodore Roosevelt's childhood home presents a startling contrast to the downtown tenements.

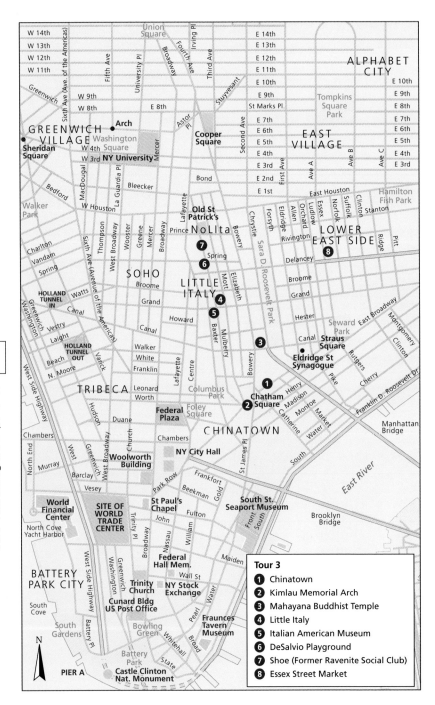

New York Immigrant Experience

W 14th
W 13th
W 12th
W 11th

Union
Square

E 14th
E 13th
E 12th
E 11th
E 10th

ALPHABET
CITY

E 10th

Greenwich

Sixth Ave (Ave. of the Americas)
Fifth Ave
University Pl
Broadway
Fourth Ave
Irving Pl
Third Ave
Stuyvesant

E 9th
St Marks Pl.

Tompkins
Square
Park

E 9th
E 8th
E 7th

W 9th
W 8th

E 8th

GREENWICH
VILLAGE

Arch

E 7th
E 6th
E 5th
E 4th
E 3rd

E 6th
E 5th
E 4th

Ave B
Ave C

Sheridan
Square

Washington
Square

Cooper
Square

EAST
VILLAGE

W 4th
W 3rd NY University

Mercer
Astor Pl
Second Ave
First Ave
Ave A

E 2nd
E 1st

Bedford

MacDougal
La Guardia Pl

Bleecker

Bond

East Houston

Hamilton
Fish Park

Walker
Park

W Houston

Lafayette

Old St
Patrick's

Chrystie
Forsyth
Eldridge
Allen
Orchard
Ludlow
Essex
Norfolk
Suffolk
Clinton
Stanton

Charlton
Vandam
Spring

Thompson
West Broadway
Wooster
Greene
Mercer
Broadway

Prince NoLIta

Rivington

LOWER
EAST SIDE

Ridge
Pitt

7
6 Spring

Delancey

8

SOHO

Broome

Elizabeth
Mott

Broome

HOLLAND
TUNNEL
IN

Sixth Ave (Avenue of the Americas)
Watts
Canal

LITTLE
ITALY

4

Grand

Grand

Hester

Sara D. Roosevelt Park

Seward
Park

East Broadway

Montgomery

Greenwich
Washington

Vestry
Laight

Howard

5

Canal

Canal

Straus
Square

Clinton

Beach
N. Moore

Varick

HOLLAND
TUNNEL
OUT

Walker
White
Franklin

Lafayette
Centre

Baxter
Mulberry

3

Bowery

Eldridge St
Synagogue

Pike

Rutgers
Cherry

West Side Highway

TRIBECA

Leonard
Worth

Columbus
Park

1

Henry
Madison
Monroe

Franklin D. Roosevelt Dr

Hudson

Duane

Federal
Plaza

Foley
Square

2 Chatham
Square

Catherine

Market

Manhattan
Bridge

Chambers

Greenwich
West
West Broadway
Church

Chambers

CHINATOWN

St James Pl
Water
South

North End
Murray
Barclay
Vesey

Woolworth
Building

NY City Hall

Park Row
Frankfort
Gold

East River

World
Financial
Center

SITE OF
WORLD
TRADE
CENTER

St Paul's
Chapel

Beekman
Fulton

South St.
Seaport Museum

Front
South

Brooklyn
Bridge

North Cove
Yacht Harbor

Trinity Pl
Broadway

John
Nassau
William

Federal
Hall Mem.

Maiden

BATTERY
PARK CITY

West Side Highway
Washington
Greenwich

Trinity
Church
Cunard Bldg
US Post Office

Wall St
NY Stock
Exchange

Water

South
Cove

Battery Park City

South
Gardens

Bowling
Green

Fraunces
Tavern
Museum

Pearl
Broad
Whitehall
State

N

Battery
Park

PIER A

Castle Clinton
Nat. Monument

Tour 3

1 Chinatown
2 Kimlau Memorial Arch
3 Mahayana Buddhist Temple
4 Little Italy
5 Italian American Museum
6 DeSalvio Playground
7 Shoe (Former Ravenite Social Club)
8 Essex Street Market

Tour 3: 1921–1970

America Closes the Golden Door

As World War I ended and American soldiers returned home, a new wave of nationalism swept the United States. Suspicion of anyone who arrived from overseas with an accent or a darker skin tone became the norm, making it uncomfortable for immigrants who sought a respite from the turmoil and destruction they had experienced in their homeland.

Congress reacted to the nationwide distrust of foreigners with a series of quota laws that sought to control the influx of immigrants. The National Origins Quota of 1924 contained two provisions: It set the annual quota of any nationality at 2 percent of the number of foreign-born persons of that nationality who were already resident in the

After World War I, quotas limited the number of immigrants entering the United States.

continental United States in 1890. In other words, if four million Italians lived in the United States in 1890, only another 80,000 could enter the country in 1924. In 1925, another 80,000 could enter, and so on.

On July 1, 1929, another, more complex stipulation took effect: First, it required the calculation of the number of immigrants from any one country in 1920. The second calculation was the percentage of immigrants from that country in relation to the entire population of the United States. So, for example, if the total population of Martians in the United States was two million, and the total population of the nation was 100 million, the percentage of Martians was 2 percent.

The calculation went on: Thus, the annual quota of people from Mars who could enter the country in a given year was 2 percent of 150,000, or 3,000 Martians. This highly restrictive quota calculation process, narrowing immigration to a trickle of its former cascade, was in effect until December 31, 1952.

Designed originally to restrict the immigration of southern and eastern Europeans, who had arrived in enormous numbers in the 1890s, the law went even further: It specifically excluded immigration of Asians and Asian Indians altogether. It also prohibited Asian men already in the United States from bringing their wives or children to join them, a prohibition begun in 1882 with the Chinese Exclusion Act.

The restrictions only began with the National Origins Quota Act, however. Late in the nineteenth century, a new interest group called the Eugenics Movement, led by Sir Francis Galton of England,

Eastern Europeans became targets of the Eugenics Movement.

trumpeted "the improvement of the human race by better breeding." The movement gained momentum in the 1920s in the United States, leading to the passage of the Johnson-Reed Act of 1924, which banned people from eastern Europe from coming into the United States. Proponents of eugenics thought that eastern Europeans were genetically inferior, and therefore should not be permitted to enter the country and pollute the American gene pool. For people already in this country who had left family members behind in hopes of earning enough to bring them to live in America, these restrictions created devastating gaps between husbands and wives, as well as between parents and their children.

As the Great Depression arrived in 1929, New York Governor Franklin Roosevelt demonstrated the kind of empathy for the lower classes that would lead to his successful run for the presidency three years later. He launched a program called Home Relief, supplying government assistance to the poor in the form of rent payment subsidies and cheese and other foods. This was the first substantial, government-run relief program in New York, and its positive effects helped keep people in their homes and off the streets, rescued families from the brink of insolvency, and fed hungry children whose parents had lost their jobs in the economic collapse.

People of some nationalities continued to build substantial populations in the United States, however, even in the face of strict quotas. Arriving just after World War I and just before the new immigration laws, Puerto Ricans established the first Latino community, known as El Barrio or Spanish Harlem, on the east side of Harlem in northern Manhattan. Sicilians had adopted this area in the late 1800s, but the influx of Latinos gradually pushed out Italian Harlem and created an entirely new ethnic neighborhood. Today, El Barrio dominates the East Harlem area.

In the 1930s, with Benito Mussolini gaining power in Italy, a new influx of Italians arrived to escape the fascist rule in their homeland, maximizing their quotas to the last man—so by 1941, there were more Italians living in the United States than in Rome, Italy. With this surge of Italian immigrants came physicists Enrico Fermi and Emilio Segrè, who became principal developers of the atom bomb; as well as future winners of the Nobel Prize in Medicine Salvador Luria and Renato Dulbecco. Symphonic conductor Arturo Toscanini also arrived in New York in the 1930s.

The world's most famous orchestral conductor, Arturo Toscanini conducted the NBC Symphony Orchestra in New York.

LaGuardia Brings Real Reform

In 1933, a first-generation American with an Italian father and an Italian-Jewish mother rose through the city's political ranks to become mayor of New York City. Fiorello LaGuardia, a major supporter of Roosevelt's New Deal who had made anti-corruption and reform the largest planks in his political platform, began the first of his three terms in office by ordering the round-up and arrest of Lucky Luciano, leader of an organized crime ring that had subjugated much of New York. With the gangsters in jail, LaGuardia went about improving the housing situation for immigrants: Among his many reforms, he passed a law that made wooden stairways illegal in buildings throughout the city, making it mandatory that these fire traps be replaced with

Steel and iron fire escapes replaced the flammable wooden stairs in the 1930s.

nonflammable materials like steel and concrete. In response, many tenement owners evicted their residents and shuttered the old buildings, a less costly alternative to expensive replacement of the stairs. This suited LaGuardia's interests—he then ordered "slum clearance," tearing down the tenements and the elevated train tracks on the Lower East Side to eliminate places for violent crime to take place. He instituted a massive public works program, administered by Parks Commissioner Robert Moses, which put thousands of poor New Yorkers— including immigrants—to work in the city's parks.

LaGuardia was one of the first Americans to speak out against Adolf Hitler, warning that part of Hitler's plan was "the complete annihilation of Jews in Germany." As World War II approached, President Franklin Roosevelt appointed the mayor as the director of the Office of Civilian Defense, an organization that took responsibility for preparing to protect the nation's civilian population in the event of an attack on America.

War, for Better or Worse

World War II brings us many of the most poignant images of the immigration experience, some of them particularly hard to view. In 1939, the SS *St. Louis,* a German transatlantic liner carrying 936 passengers—930 of them Jews—sailed from Germany for Cuba in an attempt to rescue its Jewish passengers from the genocide already in progress in their homeland. They had valid visas, but Cuba rejected them at the last moment, forcing the ship to sail for nearby Miami, Florida, in a request for asylum in America.

The SS *St. Louis* carried German Jewish refugees to the west to seek asylum.

Their request was denied, however. The Roosevelt administration chose to respect immigration law and its restrictive quotas, refusing asylum for the passengers. The SS *St. Louis* finally returned to Europe, where most of the passengers were granted asylum in the United Kingdom, France, Belgium, and the Netherlands . . . but an estimated 254 of the passengers died in German death camps during the Holocaust.

As the United States entered the war on December 8, 1941, in response to a Japanese attack on Pearl Harbor, Hawaii, the country formed an alliance with China against their mutual enemies in Japan. In light of this, the exclusion laws against Chinese immigration to America suddenly seemed out of place. Congress repealed the Chinese Exclusion Act in 1943, ending sixty-one years of legislated racial discrimination by the U.S. government. Chinese quotas were set at a very low level, however, slowing the potentially massive immigration that might have taken place during the war and its aftermath. Meanwhile, an executive order from the White House in 1942 established "war relocation camps" for Japanese-Americans and Japanese nationals throughout the West Coast, forcing thousands of people to give up their homes and wait out the war in virtual imprisonment.

In 1944, the U.S. government established the War Refugee Board, permitting civilian victims of the Nazi and Axis regimes to immigrate to America. The commission is credited with rescuing as many as 200,000 Jews from the Nazis, but by the time this board came into being, more than five million Jews had already died in the Holocaust. When the war ended and the genocide figures were fully understood, the United States had the largest surviving population of Jews in the world — about six million, nearly as many as were killed during the war.

As the war came to an end in 1945, Congress passed the War Bride Act and the GI Fiancées Act, allowing immigration of foreign-born wives, fiancées, and children of U.S. armed forces personnel. With some of the laws relaxed to allow refugees and new GI families to come to America, new nuclei of ethnic activity began to emerge in New York City — in particular, the Queens neighborhood of Astoria became a tightly knit Greek community, one that continues to thrive there today.

Immigration Enters a Modern Era

With so many people displaced from their homelands by the savagery of war, America became a favored destination for refugees — and Congress began the struggle that continues today over

The post-war mass exodus from Europe led Eastern Europeans to Ellis Island.

immigration quotas, naturalization, and the government's responsibility for noncitizens within its borders.

At war's end, countries throughout eastern Europe expelled German citizens, creating a mass exodus from the Soviet Union, Poland, Czechoslovakia, Romania, Hungary, and Yugoslavia. Many of these refugees chose the United States as their new home, swelling the quotas as they applied for admittance to a country that did not blame the entire German population for the work of the Nazi regime.

After decades of discrimination, Congress finally passed the Immigration and Nationality Act of 1952, allowing people of all races—including Asians and Asian Indians—to be eligible for naturalization. It would take another thirteen years for the last piece of legislation against the Asians to fall: the Hart-Cellar Immigration and Nationality

Act of 1965 abolished the racial quotas, permitting immigrants from China, Japan, Korea, the Philippines, India, and Vietnam to enter the United States in great numbers and become naturalized citizens. The quota for Chinese immigrants was expanded significantly in 1968, and within a few months, Chinatown began to grow as newly arrived businesspeople opened offices, garment factories, grocery stores, and fish and meat markets. In the next several years, foreign investment poured in from Hong Kong, and the area became a major tourist attraction for its authentic food from all of China's major regions, as well as its unusually affordable shopping and cultural activities. Most recently, Chinatown's growth and popularity have spiked apartment rental rates to unprecedented levels that rival the Upper West Side and Midtown,

With the ban lifted on Chinese immigration, Chinatown began to grow.

while the city-within-a-city continues to expand into the traditionally Italian and Jewish neighborhoods that flank it on every side.

1. Chinatown. About 40 percent of Lower Manhattan residents are of Chinese descent, and the recent explosive growth of Chinatown demonstrates the strength and cohesion of this population in New York. It's the food and the shopping that make this area such a treat for visitors.

Open-air markets with exotic fruits and vegetables abound in Chinatown.

Since food and travel writers for newspapers and magazines discovered the wonders of Chinese food in the 1890s, tourists have come to this area to feast on delicacies from eight different regions: Anhui, Guangdong (where Cantonese cuisine originates), Fujian, Hunan, Jiangsu, Shandong, Sichuan (where Szechuan cuisine originates), and Zhejiang, all easy to locate on restaurant signs on the town's crowded streets. Fresh fruits and vegetables you may not have encountered in your local supermarket—like dragon fruit and lychee—heap up on outdoor carts and wooden produce stands at open-air markets, while the herbs, roots, and other natural elements of traditional Chinese medicine are readily available in exotic grocery stores. Tourists can buy authentically Asian gifts or designer knockoff scarves and handbags, most at the cheapest prices you'll find anywhere. Current borders are, roughly, Hester Street to the north, Broadway on the west, Worth Street to the south, and the Bowery on the east, with single streets featuring Chinese merchants and restaurants beyond these boundaries; www.nyctourist.com/chinatown1.htm or www.chinatown-online.com. Stores tend to close after 10 p.m., restaurants may be open past midnight. CHINATOWN

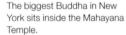
Find the Kimlau Arch in Chatham Square.

2. Kimlau Memorial Arch. Seven roads lead to this square, where a huge stone ceremonial arch commemorates World War II fighter pilot Benjamin Ralph Kimlau and all of the Chinese-Americans lost in the war. Also here is a statue of Lin Ze Xu, the 1839 Qing Dynasty official who worked to stop imperialists from bringing opium into China. Despite his best efforts, the consequences of China's resistance led to the Opium War, followed by the ceding of Hong Kong to Great Britain. Chatham Square, www.nycgovparks.org/parks/M246/. Always open. Free. CHINATOWN

3. Mahayana Buddhist Temple. At the foot of the Manhattan Bridge, this huge temple holds the 16-foot-tall gold Buddha you came to Chinatown to see. The red lacquered doors and big gold lions out front make this temple easy to spot. You'd never guess that before 1996, this building was a pornographic movie theater. 133 Canal Street, (212) 925-8787. Daily 8–6. Free (buy your fortune for $1). CHINATOWN

New York Immigrant Experience

The biggest Buddha in New York sits inside the Mahayana Temple.

4. Little Italy. This vibrant neighborhood offers dozens of restaurants, boutiques, and bakeries that bring the flavors of Italy's various regions to the table and the street. In spring, summer, and early fall, Little Italy's merchants and restaurants take to the sidewalks, creating a daily and nightly Italian bazaar with al fresco dining, kitschy shopping, twinkling lights, and ethnic music. Come hungry! The street is always open; merchants begin to open early in the morning and close when the crowds subside at night. Concentrated in just a few blocks on Mulberry Street: south to Canal Street and north to Spring Street, www.littleitaly nyc.com. LITTLE ITALY

It's a perpetual street fair on Mulberry Street, the heart of Little Italy.

5. Italian American Museum. This small museum is on the verge of major growth, with the purchase of several adjacent buildings in Little Italy. At this writing, it houses an exhibition of objects, artifacts, and correspondence relating to Italian immigration and life in America. Don't miss the translation of a real extortion letter from the early 1900s, or the fabulous marionette built and painted in the old country. 155 Mulberry Street, (212) 965-9000, www.italianamericanmuseum.org. Wed, Tues, Sat, Sun, 11–6, Fri 11–8; closed Mon and Tues. $5 suggested donation. LITTLE ITALY

6. DeSalvio Playground. First-generation American John DeSalvio became a local prizefighting champion in the welterweight division before retiring from boxing to open a saloon at 202 Hester Street. He went on to become district leader of the Second Assembly District and worked his way into the Tammany Hall organization as one of the only Italians ever permitted membership; later,

This playground commemorates John DeSalvio, an Italian philanthropist.

he opened a classy restaurant and nightclub and used a portion of his proceeds to pay bills for his poorest neighbors. His son, Louis, also became a member of the New York State Assembly. This playground, with a fountain that's a big hit with the neighborhood children, honors the achievements of two men who devoted their careers to the people of Little Italy. Corner of Mulberry and Spring Streets, www.nycgovparks.org/parks/M218/. Always open. Free. LITTLE ITALY

7. Site of the Ravenite Social Club (now Shoe). Nothing remains of the former hangout frequented by mob boss John Gotti Jr. and the Gambino crime family, but you can still imagine the complexity and stealth of the major FBI wiretapping operation that recorded Gotti's conversations with his cronies in this building. The information

Shoe replaced the Ravenite Social Club, where the FBI caught up with John Gotti Jr.

gathered here helped send Gotti to prison in 1992, where he lived out his days until his death in 2002. Today the building is a shoe store called Shoe (212-925-1735, www.bagandshoe.com; daily 12–7), carrying its own branded designer shoes for men and women, as well as belts and handbags. 247 Mulberry Street. LITTLE ITALY

8. Essex Street Market. Established by Mayor LaGuardia to clear streets on the Lower East Side and bring pushcart vendors indoors in a central location, this shopping center houses several fresh-food grocers, two restaurants, and merchants who offer imported goods, health foods, and more exotic ingredients. 120 Essex Street, (212) 388-0449, www.essexstreetmarket.com. Mon–Sat 8–7; closed Sun. Free to browse; most merchants accept credit cards, but some only take cash. LOWER EAST SIDE

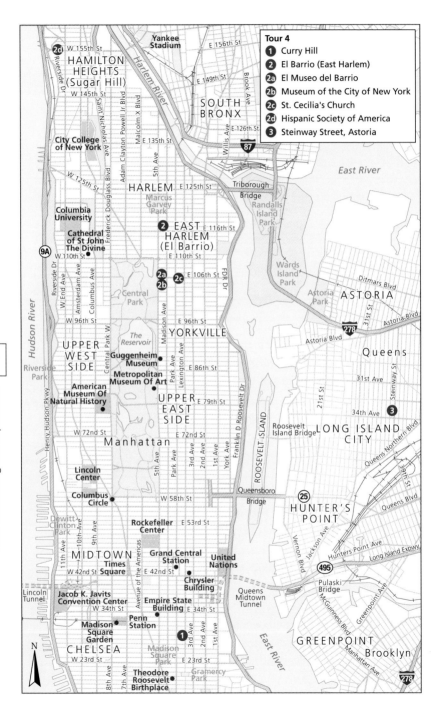

New York Immigrant Experience

Tour 4
1. Curry Hill
2. El Barrio (East Harlem)
2a. El Museo del Barrio
2b. Museum of the City of New York
2c. St. Cecilia's Church
2d. Hispanic Society of America
3. Steinway Street, Astoria

Tour 4: 1971–Present

Immigration: A Never-Ending Story

As a period of relative peace came to Europe with
the end of the Cold War, dissolution of the Soviet
Union, a peace agreement between England and
Northern Ireland, and war's end in the Bosnia-
Herzegovina region, European immigration slowed
to a trickle in New York City. The U.S. Census tells
a compelling story: In 1970, the census revealed
that foreign-born residents were mostly from (in
descending order) Italy, Poland, the Soviet Union,
Germany, Ireland, Cuba, the Dominican Republic, the United Kingdom, Australia, and Jamaica.
By 2000, the complexion in New York literally
changed: Foreign-born residents primarily hailed
from the Dominican Republic, China, Jamaica,
Mexico, Guyana, Ecuador, Haiti, Trinidad and
Tobago, India, and Colombia.

The transition happened gradually. An influx
of Soviet Jews arrived in the 1980s to escape the
religious persecution their government mandated.
In 1980, the census proved that New York City's
Chinatown housed the largest concentration of
Chinese-Americans in the United States, topping
cities including San Francisco and Los Angeles.
As the turn of the century approached, however,
Asians and Hispanic/Latino populations became
the largest immigrant communities, filling neighborhoods vacated by Europeans and their descendants as they moved on to the suburbs of Queens
and Brooklyn. We find primarily Latino neighborhoods in El Barrio (Spanish Harlem) at the north

Summer street fairs unite many ethnicities on one thoroughfare.

end of Manhattan; collections of Latinos and Caribbeans on the Lower East Side; thousands of Dominicans centered in Washington Heights, an immigration spurred by political unrest in the 1960s and rampant poverty since then; and Asian Indians coming together in downtown Manhattan. The city's annual Philippines Independence Day celebration, on Madison Avenue on the first Sunday in June, brings tens of thousands of Filipino nationals and their children to central Manhattan for an extensive, three-hour parade and a 27-block street fair. More than 215,000 Filipinos have arrived since the abolishment of quotas in 1965, most bringing their professional skills as doctors, nurses, accountants, and engineers to their new country. On any summer weekend, street fairs highlighting a dozen nationalities close entire thoroughfares to traffic, turning an area into a perpetual international party.

Today what we think of as the traditional, primarily European immigrant populations live primarily in Queens (36.2 percent) and Brooklyn (31.4 percent), while only 14.7 percent live in Manhattan. Meanwhile, New Yorkers of Hispanic descent grew from 16.3 percent of the population in 1970 to 19.9 percent in 1980 to 24.4 percent in 1990. As many as 200,000 Mexican nationals now live in the five-borough area, while Dominicans have outpaced Puerto Ricans as the city's largest Hispanic group. In addition, New York City has the largest population of black immigrants in the country: more than 686,000 from Jamaica, Trinidad and Tobago, Barbardos, Guyana, Belize, Grenada, and Haiti. A much smaller group emigrated from sub-Saharan Africa.

With all of the citizens of other nations who have come to America to seek their fortune, however, one group still holds the top spot for number of nationals and descendants living in New York City: More than 3.3 million Italians inhabit the New York metropolitan area. It's no wonder, then, that Columbus Day is a major holiday in New York, and that Mulberry Street becomes a five-block fête every September 19 for the Feast of San Gennaro. Not to be outdone, the Sicilians celebrate Santa Rosalita every year on September 4.

With 3.3 million Italians living in New York, specialty shops like Alleva do brisk business.

Diversity is everywhere in New York—no longer concentrated in a corner of Manhattan, but spread liberally throughout the city. Your cab drivers, horse-drawn carriage drivers, waiters, street vendors, shopkeepers, grocers, and many more are immigrants or first-generation Americans, and you'll hear a dozen different languages spoken on the street in just a few blocks' walk.

Focus your exploration of modern-day cultural diversity on one or more of the following areas, each with its distinctive ethnic mix of food, drink, shopping, and community centers. Whichever you choose, plan to make a day of it—there is a lot to see, eat, and shop for in each of these fascinating neighborhoods.

Murray Hill is now Curry Hill, a concentration of Indian and Pakistani restaurants.

1. Curry Hill. You'll smell the Indian spices as you come up from the subway; the Murray Hill neighborhood got its "Curry Hill" nickname because it holds a remarkable concentration of Indian and Pakistani restaurants, shops, and grocery stores. In just a couple of blocks, you'll have the opportunity to try Indian cuisine from several different regions, from southern India to Gujarat, as well as vegetarian "mock meat" specialties that are certified kosher, and the relatively new Chinese-Indian hybrid dishes. Lexington Avenue between 27th and 29th Streets. Stores are open by 10 a.m. and keep regular business hours; walking and window-shopping are free.

2. El Barrio (Spanish Harlem or East Harlem). Nearly 120,000 Latinos live here today, arrivals from Central and South America, Mexico, and the Caribbean islands. While the neighborhood itself remains low-income, it features a host of restaurants with all manner of dishes born of localized cuisine, and plenty of places to find all kinds of items in Spanish. Bounded by Harlem River (north), East River (east), East 96th Street (south), 5th Avenue (west), www.east-harlem.com.

Don't miss these venues as you explore El Barrio:

- **El Museo del Barrio.** New York's premier Caribbean and Latin American cultural institution, El Museo presents a solid representation of the diversity of art and culture in the Caribbean and Latin America. Founded in 1969 by artist and educator Raphael Montañez Ortiz and a group of community activists, educators, artists, and parents, it has since evolved into one of the leading Latino and Latin American museums in the nation. 1230 Fifth Avenue at 104th Street, (212) 831-7272, www.elmuseo.org. Wed–Sun 11–5; closed Mon–Tues. Adults $6, students and seniors $4, children under 12 free.

- **Museum of the City of New York.** Just across the street from El Museo, this museum is a treat—the one place in town where you'll find the narrative of the Dutch conquest of New

See how uptown folks lived by visiting the Museum of the City of New York.

Netherland in the 1600s. Permanent exhibitions provide one of the city's only lingering looks at the upscale homes and furnishings of New York's well-to-do. 1220 Fifth Avenue, at 103rd Street, (212) 534-1672, www.mcny.org. Tues–Sun 10–5. Adults $10, seniors and students $6, children under 12 free.

St. Cecilia's Church is a central landmark in El Barrio.

- **St. Cecilia's Roman Catholic Church (Parroquia Sta. Cecilia).** This beautiful church was dedicated as an Italian house of worship in 1873; today it serves the Dominican, Puerto Rican, and Cuban populations in this neighborhood. 125 East 105th Street, (212) 534-1350. Open for mass daily at 7, 8:15, and 12:10 p.m., Sun at 8, 9:45, and 11:30 a.m., with many services in Spanish. Free.

- **Hispanic Society of America.** Perhaps the most comprehensive survey in the United States of the arts and culture of Spain, Portugal, and Latin America, this museum features more than 800 paintings and 6,000 watercolors and drawings from the Middle Ages to present day. In addition, nearly a thousand works of sculpture and thousands of art objects—jewelry, furniture, textiles, and glass—round out the extraordinary collection. 613 West 155th St. (Audubon Terrace), at Broadway, (212) 926-2234, www .hispanicsociety.org. Tues–Sat 10–4:30, Sun 1–4; closed Mon. Free.

3. Steinway Street in Astoria, Queens. The recent emergence of a growing Middle Eastern population has turned this road into a vibrant strip of groceries, restaurants, shops, and services run by people of Arabic, Iranian, Lebanese, Turkish, and other northern African descent. The established Greek population maintains its presence on Steinway and the numbered cross streets, while a Brazilian flavor has begun to arrive here as well. Check the papers for listings of summer street fairs, where you'll find vendors of Indian, Mexican, and Cuban descent among the Middle Eastern and Mediterranean immigrants.

Buy a hookah (or smoke from one provided) on Astoria's Steinway Street.

Downtown New York City: A Tourist's Guide to Staying, Eating, and Exploring

Whether you're exploring the Lower East Side neighborhood to discover your family's immigration story, or you just love ethnic neighborhoods and the unusual shopping and dining experiences they offer, you can have a wonderful time in parts of the city most tourists won't stumble upon on their own. Fifty blocks away from the Broadway theater district and miles from Bloomingdale's and Saks Fifth Avenue, you'll find that prices come back into line with what mere mortals pay for their clothing and meals, and haute couture relaxes into jeans, T-shirts, and comfortable walking shoes.

The casual hip that you sense here belies an underlying trend that's bringing upscale change to one of New York's oldest districts. Thanks to a recent migration of young urban professionals into the Lower East Side, many of the old, dilapidated buildings that were barely a step past tenements have been transformed into carefully improved lofts and apartments, significantly upgraded with modern utilities and restored architectural details. Where young professionals with disposable income choose to live, trendy bars, shops, and restaurants quickly follow, making the Lower East Side—also known as the LES—a whole lot more fashionable than its original inhabitants could imagine. Plenty of low-income residents still make their homes here, but it's a prettier LES than your mother or grandmother might remember.

Not only are the slums of the 1800s and early

1900s long gone, but the sense of unease that visitors experienced thirty years ago in this area is absent as well. Ask any of the residents, and they are quick to credit Mayor Rudolph Giuliani's policies for "cleaning up" New York. It's true that Mayor Rudy increased the size of the police force, cleared the streets of homeless people (for the most part), and created a less trashy, more family-friendly city—and whatever you may feel about

You'll find fresh produce, health foods, and affordable shopping at Essex Street Market.

his methods or his politics, it's hard to argue with the result. From the Alphabet Streets to the Bowery, Lower Manhattan feels like a safe place to be, and the streets are crowded with working people, tourists, street vendors, and shops with sidewalk stalls from early morning until well after dark.

Take the usual precautions when you visit New York, just as you would in any major city: Stay alert to the people around you, keep your valuables out of sight, don't leave your belongings unattended, and stick to well-lit streets where there are plenty of other folks. Don't panic if a stranger starts to talk to you—Lower Manhattan is loaded with friendly people who will suggest restaurants, point you in the right direction toward the subway station, and engage you in a kibbitz at a moment's notice.

If you don't know the city well, carry a map or a GPS device to help you find your way around; remember that twenty north-to-south city blocks in New York equal about a mile, while the blocks going east to west are longer.

Most important, leave your car at home and take full advantage of New York's excellent mass-transit system. Parking your car in Manhattan can

run as much as $25 per hour, and while you will
find less expensive parking garages in Lower Manhattan, these fill up quickly, especially during the
work week. Worse, driving your vehicle means that
you will spend a great deal of your valuable time
sitting in traffic and circling the block looking for
parking spaces, when you could be strolling down
Mott Street, window-shopping, and munching on
almond cookies or steamed pork buns.

Subways run on time fairly consistently, and
they're a cheap, clean, and reasonably comfortable
way to get from downtown to uptown in a short
amount of time (for example, the subway can get
you from Grand Central Terminal to Bowling Green,
the stop for Battery Park, in under fifteen minutes).
The days of tokens or change are gone—buy a
MetroCard at any subway station from one of the
easy-to-use vending machines, and pay with cash
or a credit/debit card. One ride is $2.25, whether
you take the subway (north/south) or a city bus
(east/west), and you can choose a 7-day Unlimited
Ride MetroCard and ride as many times as you like
until midnight on your seventh day. More information on fares, routes, and schedules is available at
www.mta.info.

WHERE TO STAY IN LOWER MANHATTAN

It's no secret that hotel rooms in Manhattan are
some of the most expensive in the country, but
the farther you get from Midtown, the more likely
you are to find truly special accommodations at
a reasonable price. Most recently, the Lower East
Side has experienced a boom in "boutique" hotels,
independently owned enterprises with exclusive

styling and amenities you may not run into at the chain hotels.

Many of the hotels listed here provide just that kind of encounter, products of an enlightened hotelier's ideas and tastes in everything from bed linens to custom-scented soap and lotion. Elegance comes with a price, but the splurge is less painful when the experience is off the scale.

Blue Moon Hotel, 100 Orchard Street, (212) 533-9080, www.bluemoon-nyc.com. Just down the street from the Lower East Side Tenement Museum, this delightful boutique hotel brings together the building's original details with the modern amenities we expect in the twenty-first century. The result is a luxurious hotel with a sense of history, visible in the painstakingly restored architectural elements. Satellite television, DVD players, and Wi-Fi in every room make this an especially nice place from which to enjoy Lower Manhattan. LOWER EAST SIDE

Blue Moon offers a boutique hotel experience with a sense of history.

The Bowery Hotel, 335 Bowery, (212) 505-9100, www.theboweryhotel.com. The lobby's luxurious, nineteenth-century Irish decor may lead you to

The new Bowery Hotel brings old-world charm to Lower Manhattan.

believe that this is a historic hotel, but The Bowery opened in 2007—which means plenty of modern amenities, contemporary rooms, and a choice of queen or king beds, suites, or a one-bedroom (a 1,275-foot suite that's larger than many New York apartments). The red-accented rooms feature Egyptian cotton linens, marble bathrooms, toiletries by C.O. Bigelow. and high-definition television—and with 24-hour room service, turndown service, a daily newspaper, and a complimentary DVD library, you hardly need to go out. DOWNTOWN

Cooper Square Hotel, 25 Cooper Square, (888) 847-4869, www.thecoopersquarehotel.com. The latest in concept hotels, Cooper Square shuns the usual check-in desk, replacing it with a chat with a host or hostess over a complimentary beverage while your registration is completed. Once inside, the glass, chrome, and soft gray-and-black interior design—carried through even in the clothing of the young, genial staff members, who receive impeccable training in customer service—all bespeak the one-of-a-kind hotel experience to come. Your room provides an unobstructed, ceiling-to-floor view of Manhattan, while surrounding you with

The ultra-modern Cooper Square Hotel offers comfort, luxury, and terrific Manhattan skyline views.

neutral gray and white tones and ultramodern styling. Even the toiletries are unique to this hotel, with a scent designed specifically for Cooper Square. It's pricey, but for a special vacation or a peak experience trip, it's worth it. EAST VILLAGE

Hotel East Houston, 151 East Houston Street, (212) 777-0012, www.hoteleasthouston.com. Renovated in 2007, this stylish boutique hotel offers a number of amenities that make up for the smaller rooms, from sleek bedding and Bulgari toiletries to free breakfast and Wi-Fi. The best part is the rooftop deck, a lounge area with a killer view of the city's famous skyline. LOWER EAST SIDE

The newly renovated Hotel East Houston has a rooftop deck with a terrific view.

Hotel 91, 91 East Broadway, (646) 438-6600, www.hotel91.com. A recent entry into Lower Manhattan's boutique hotel collection, Hotel 91 offers reasonably priced rooms by New York standards, with bathrooms lined in marble, pillow-top beds, and that new marvel in modern accommodations: silent climate control (no air conditioner buzzing in the middle of the night). Luscious all-white bed linens and cozy comforters are the last touch in this ultra-modern, uncluttered hotel, where a dash of Asian design sensibility lends serenity to each room. LOWER EAST SIDE

Hotel 91 offers proximity to Chinatown in a boutique atmosphere.

Hotel on Rivington, 107 Rivington Street, (212) 475-2600, (800) 915-1537, www.hotelonrivington .com. That twenty-one-story glass tower standing between hundred-year-old brick buildings is a concept hotel its management calls "a celebration of creative energy." Guests benefit from the floor-to-ceiling windows in every room with unobstructed views of Manhattan, a private lobby and lounge, and beds with Swedish memory-foam mattresses topped with Frette linens. Ask for a room with a "shower with a view." LOWER EAST SIDE

Off Soho Suites, 11 Rivington Street, (800) 633-7646, www.offsoho.com. Recently remodeled, this older hotel has a new, modern look in its comfortably roomy suites, each of which features a fully equipped kitchen. In addition to the excellent location, this hotel offers unusually affordable rates without skimping on the amenities: free high-speed Internet, a fitness center, and a coin laundry. LOWER EAST SIDE

WHERE TO EAT IN LOWER MANHATTAN

When last we checked, there were more than 6,500 restaurants in New York City, each with a story to tell and a specialty of the house. With the help of the locals—friends, coworkers, and people we met on the street—we've put together a list of eateries on the Lower East Side, in Chinatown and Little Italy, and tucked away in other corners, each of which provides an authentic ethnic experience, a smattering of history, and a truly great meal, dessert, or walkabout snack.

No meat? No problem for Buddha Bodai Vegetarian on Mott Street.

Buddha Bodai Vegetarian Restaurant, 5 Mott Street, at Mosco Street and Chatham Square, (212) 566-8388, www.buddhabodai.com. You won't miss the meat—these purveyors of "mock meat" are wizards in their brilliant emulation of meat's texture, appearance, and taste, all created using only plant-based foods. General Tso's chicken tastes enough like the real thing to make you forget you're eating a clever combination of beans and soy, and the shrimp dumpling is indistinguishable from the authentic sea critter. Tasty and affordable—the best combination. Daily 10:30 a.m.–11 p.m. CHINATOWN

Economy Candy, 108 Rivington Street, at Essex Street, (212) 254-1531, www.economycandy.com. Think of your favorite candy from days of yore: Pixy Stix? Teaberry gum? Chocolate Ice Cubes? They're all here, and hundreds more besides, in this chockablock candy emporium. If you've got a hankering for fresh halvah, they've got that as well—along with all the character Pez dispensers, lots of premium chocolates, a wide selection of sugar-free varieties, gift baskets, and seasonal items from hamantaschen to chocolate Santas. Get your single-color M&M's here in bulk. Sun–Fri 9–6, Sat 10–5. LOWER EAST SIDE

Find your favorite old-time confection at Economy Candy.

Grotto Azzurra, 177 Mulberry Street, (212) 925-8775, www.grottaazzurrany.com. This outstanding restaurant enjoyed a recent rebirth after six years of silence, and now returns to the high style of its 1908 origins. Once a favorite of opera star Enrico Caruso, and the top choice of Frank Sinatra and his Rat Pack posse, Grotto Azzurra now serves specialties as pleasantly simple as *maiale scallopini* (pork in an herb-laden wine sauce) or spaghetti *polpettine* (with meatballs), or as original as *braciole di manzo,* a stuffed beef concoction with herbs, Parmesan, and prosciutto. If you can't make it for dinner, stop in for breakfast. Daily 7:30 a.m.–12 a.m. LITTLE ITALY

Il Cortile, 125 Mulberry Street, (212) 226-6060, www.ilcortile.com. Well off the beaten path of Italian menu offerings, Il Cortile takes traditional entrées and gives each an ingenious twist, filling gnocchi with chicken, spinach, and mascarpone cheese or dressing up chicken marsala with a mushroom, prosciutto, onion and mozzarella stuffing. Even the antipasti push past the norm, with stuffed Cubanelle peppers, a bruschetta that features fava beans, and *scacciata di salsaicce e carciofi,* a pie involving artichokes, sausage, and mozzarella. It's no wonder that Danny DeVito got married here, and that Billy Joel was inspired to write "Scenes from an Italian Restaurant" while overhearing a conversation during a meal at Il Cortile. Sun–Thurs 12 p.m.–12 a.m., Fri–Sat 12 p.m.–1 a.m.; closed Mon. LITTLE ITALY

Joe's Shanghai, 9 Pell Street, (212) 233-8888, www.joeshanghairestaurants.com. Here's something you won't see every day: soup dumplings—Chinese dumplings crafted from a Shanghai recipe, filled with a delicious broth as well as a crab or pork meatball. An order of eight will serve as lunch, and their slurpy goodness makes them great fun to eat. If you still need an entrée, have no fear—the menu features many of your traditional Chinese favorites, as well as some creative treatment of prawns that will delight your palate. Daily 11 a.m.–11 p.m. CHINATOWN

Katz's Delicatessen, 205 East Houston Street, (212) 254-2246, www.katzdeli.com. It's been here since 1888, and the proprietors of the most authentically Jewish delicatessen in New York still prepare and preserve the meat the way it's been done for hundreds of years. The result is the best pastrami you've ever tasted, as well as a damn fine plate of pickles, fresh breads, and baked goods, and the opportunity to sit where Meg Ryan sat when she had that legendary fake orgasm in *When Harry Met Sally.* Have a nosh and an egg cream alongside members of New York's Finest— who know the best places in town to eat—and any number of celebrities who seek this place out whenever they're in New York. Sun, Wed, Thurs 8 a.m.–10:45 p.m., Mon and Tues 8 a.m.–9:45 p.m, Fri and Sat 8 a.m.–2:45 p.m. LOWER EAST SIDE

At Katz's, the deli masters stack the pastrami thick and high.

Kossar's Bialys, 367 Grand Street, (212) 253-2146, 877-424-2597, www.kossarsbialys.com. For hand-crafted, old world-style bialys—rounds of dough that surround a filling of ground onion paste—there's nowhere like Kossar's, where the bakers bring more than half a century's experience to their craft. The store added bagels to its offerings in 1998, and these kettle-boiled baked goods are among the best in New York— no small achievement in the city that put the bagel on the national culinary map. Stop in for a nosh, and take home a dozen. Sun–Thurs 6 a.m.–8 p.m., Fri 6 a.m.–3 p.m.; closed Sat. LOWER EAST SIDE.

La Bella Ferrara Pasticceria, 108 Mulberry Street, between Canal and Hester Streets, (212) 966-7867, www.littleitalynyc.com/labellaferrara. Wherever you dine in Little Italy, leave room for some cookies, cannoli, or cake at this wonderful little bakery. A startling variety of Italian pastries range from those little cookies by the pound to a sweetly

Biscotti, canoli, or butter cookies—you won't go wrong at La Bella Ferrara.

stuffed chocolate-mousse cannoli. Doesn't everyone need a tiramisu napoleon to top off a night in Lower Manhattan? Sun–Thurs 9 a.m.–midnight, Fri 9 a.m.–1 a.m., Sat 9 a.m.–2 a.m. LITTLE ITALY

McSorley's Old Ale House, 15 East 7th Street, near Astor Place, (212) 474-9148, www.mcsorleys newyork.com. The oldest continually operating Irish bar in New York was founded in 1854, and revelers still pack the place on a nightly basis. The no-frills barroom, the large wooden tables where you may find yourself seated with a group of people you didn't know when you came in, and the two-for-one mugs of the house brew—ale or lager—make this gem of the old world a casual delight. Plus, they serve a tasty burger and a good, hearty sandwich—check the chalkboard as you enter for the day's specials. Mon–Sat 11 a.m.–1 p.m., Sun 1 p.m.–1 a.m. DOWNTOWN

Stop for an ale or a lager at McSorley's, the oldest continually operating Irish bar in New York.

New York Immigrant Experience

Positano Ristorante, 122 Mulberry Street, (212) 334-9808. The light, rustic plaster decor with terra-cotta details provides just enough of a sense of Italy to raise expectations about the food—and the homemade pastas served al dente, real Caesar salad, and flavorful sauces meet those expectations with honors. Locals insisted that we stop here, and we are grateful that they did. Daily 12 p.m.–12 a.m. LITTLE ITALY

Vanessa's Dumpling House, 118 Eldridge Street, between Grand and Broome Streets, (212) 625-8008. Dumplings and big sesame pancakes are all that Vanessa's does, so it stands to reason that it would have some of the best dumplings in Chinatown. Boiled or fried, these morsels serve up fresh, hot and delicious—try the basil and chicken, or the dumpling of the month. The sesame pancake wedges are stuffed with sandwich fixings from Peking duck to tuna salad, a terrific alternative to that same boring ham on rye. Daily 7:30 a.m.–9:30 p.m. CHINATOWN

The handmade dumplings are divine at Vanessa's.

Veselka, 9th Street and 2nd Avenue, (212) 228-9682, www.veselka.com. What's Ukrainian soul food? Find out at this deceptively understated coffee shop, where the veal goulash is as good as it sounds, and traditional dishes include stuffed cabbage, kielbasa, Ukrainian meatballs in a creamy mushroom sauce, and *bigos*—the kind of meaty stew you want on a snowy day. Be sure to leave room for the baked chocolate custard—so rich, it's like eating whipped fudge. Daily 24 hours. EAST VILLAGE

Dessert at Veselka is loaded with Eastern European goodness.

You need a knish from the world-famous Yonah Schimmel's.

Yonah Schimmel Knishery, 137 East Houston Street, between 1st and 2nd Avenues, (212) 477-2858, www.knishery.com. You've never had a knish? Rectify that situation at Schimmel's, where the baked concoctions are the best you'll find in New York—with a wide variety of flavors you won't see in your home deli. Potato, kasha, and spinach are the staples, but the menu only begins here: Try the red cabbage knish for a tangy treat, or the sweet-potato knish for a genuinely American fusion experience. If you're stopping after dinner at Katz's, pick up a dessert knish here—choose from apple, blueberry, cherry, or chocolate, each combined with a cheesecake-like filling. Top it off with an egg cream, and you've truly experienced New York. Sun–Thurs 9 a.m.–7 p.m., Fri–Sat 9 a.m–10 p.m. LOWER EAST SIDE

Dine al fresco at Zum Schneider in Alphabet City.

Zum Schneider, 107 Avenue C at East 7th Street, (212) 598-1098, www.zumschneider.com. When the menu begins with an appetizer of herring in cream sauce, you know you're in for something special—and the German food at Zum gets its authenticity from the Bavarian owner. *Schweinebraten* (pork in a dark beer gravy) and *zwiebelrostbraten* (sirloin in red wine sauce) are just two of the hearty features; don't forget the side of *spätzle* (pasta) or *krautsalat* (cabbage salad). Choose from a wide selection of German beers and wines. Opens Mon–Thurs at 5, Fri at 4, Sat–Sun at 1; closing times in the wee hours, depending on the crowd. EAST VILLAGE

WHERE TO EAT BEYOND LOWER MANHATTAN

Bohemian Hall & Beer Garden, 29–12 24th Avenue, at 29th Street, Queens. (718) 274-4925, www.bohemianhall.com. Once upon a time New York City boasted dozens of beer gardens, but this Queens establishment is one of the only ones that remain. The eastern European fare features potato pierogies, Czech potato pancakes, grilled *kolbasa* (kielbasa), chicken schnitzel, and plenty more, as well as an impressive collection of Czech and Slavic beers. Word to the wise: Call ahead; this is a popular place for private parties, so be sure the beer garden is open before you go. Restaurant Mon–Wed 5–10 p.m., Thurs–Fri 5–11 p.m., Sat–Sun 12 p.m.–11 p.m. Bar and garden Mon–Wed and Sun 12 p.m.–2 a.m., Thurs–Sat 12 p.m.–3 a.m. ASTORIA.

The *arroz con pollo* is unbeatable at La Fonda Boricua.

La Fonda Boricua, 169 East 106th Street, between 3rd and Lexington Avenues, (212) 410-7292, www.fondaboricua.com. Head uptown to Spanish Harlem for home-style Puerto Rican cooking in a restaurant with no printed menus— the chef uses the day's freshest ingredients to plan lunch and dinner. Stews, steaks, and roasted pork may be on the board, along with *mofongo,* a concoction of fried green plantains or yucca, mashed with garlic and pork cracklings. Best of all is chef Jorge Ayala's *arroz con pollo* (chicken with rice), which beat a challenge from celebrity chef Bobby Flay (documented on his Food Network TV show *Throwdown! with Bobby Flay*), who thought he could make it better. He couldn't. Daily 11–9. EL BARRIO (SPANISH HARLEM)

Staying, Eating, and Exploring

Glossary

Ashkenazi: Jews who came from Eastern Europe and Russia. Eastern European Jews developed their own language—Yiddish—and became the largest contingent of the Jewish faith to come to America.

diaspora: Originally, this referred to the scattering of Jews to countries outside of the Palestine region in sixth century BC. Today, any group migration from a country or region can be called a diaspora (dispersion); the word may also refer to a religious population living as a minority among those of other religions.

emigrate: To move away from a place, especially your native country, to live in another country.

eugenics: Belief in improving the qualities of the human species by selective breeding, essentially breeding out genetic defects by not allowing "imperfect" individuals to mate and bear children.

immigration: The act of entering another country for the purpose of settling there on a permanent basis.

kibbitz: A Yiddish word, meaning "chat."

landsmanschaftn: Support organizations for people who came from the same region or town, particularly in communities of German or Jewish immigrants.

nativism: A belief that only people who were born in a country should have rights or power in that country.

naturalization: The act of a foreign national earning and/or being granted citizenship in an adopted country.

New York City metropolitan area: The twenty-three counties around New York's five boroughs are all considered part of the New York City metropolitan area. This includes ten counties in New York State, twelve in northern and central New Jersey, and one in northeastern Pennsylvania. The New York metropolitan area has more than eighteen million residents.

Rosh Hashanah: The Jewish New Year, celebrated for two days in September based on the Jewish calendar.

Sephardic: Jews whose ancestry originated on the Iberian Peninsula (Spain and Portugal). Some scholars also include Jews who were part of the Islamic world along the Mediterranean Sea, in Asia, Africa, and the Middle East as Sephardim.

Shabbos: The Jewish Sabbath, celebrated from sundown on Friday to sundown on Saturday.

Yom Kippur: The Jewish Day of Atonement, observed eight days after the first day of Rosh Hashanah.

Bibliography

Anbinder, Tyler. *Five Points: The 19th-Century New York City Neighborhood that Invented Tap Dance, Stole Elections, and Became the World's Most Notorious Slum.* New York: Plume, 2002.

Burrows, Edwin G. and Mike Wallace. *Gotham: A History of New York City to 1898.* Oxford, England: Oxford University Press, 1999.

Christiano, Gregory J. Urbanography "1857—A Year to Forget: An Introduction to a Turbulent Period of New York City History." http://urbanography.com/1857.

Harris, Leslie M. *In the Shadow of Slavery: African Americans in New York City, 1626–1863.* Chicago: University of Chicago Press, 2002.

Hubbard, Elbert. *A.T. Stewart: Little Journeys To The Homes Of Forgotten Business Men.* Vol. 25, no. 4. East Aurora, NY: The Roycrofters, 1909.

Lower East Side Tenement Museum National Historic Site Web site, http://www.tenement.org.

The New York Times, various articles.

Paine, Albert B. *Th. Nast, His Period and His Pictures.* Princeton: Pyne Press, 1904.

Polland, Annie. *Landmark of the Spirit: The Eldridge Street Synagogue.* New Haven: Yale University Press, 2008.

New York Immigrant Experience

Powell, Kimberly. "Meet the Real Ellis Island Annie," Kimberly's Genealogy Blog, About .com, September 16, 2006, http://genealogy .about.com/b/2006/09/16/meet-the-real-ellis-island-annie.htm

Roosevelt, Theodore. *New York: A Sketch of the City's Social, Political and Commercial Progress from the First Dutch Settlement to Recent Times.* New York: Charles Scribner's Sons, 1906. www.bartleby.com/171/.

United States Department of the Interior. "Tenement Building at 97 Orchard Street," National Register of Historic Places Registration Form, October 8, 1993. www.nps.gov/history/nhl/ Tenement%20Building.pdf.

U.S. Department of State Under Secretary for Public Diplomacy and Public Affairs. "Chinese Immigration and the Chinese Exclusion Acts." http://www.state.gov/r/pa/ho/time/gp/82014 .htm.

Wiley & Putnam's Emigrant's Guide. Fort Washington, Pa.: Wiley & Putnam, 2007. First published 1845 by Wiley & Putnam.

Index

New York Immigrant Experience

Index

New York Immigrant Experience